Canoeing the Indian Way

Canoeing the Indian Way

Straight Talk for Modern Paddlers
from the Dean of American Canoeists

Pierre Pulling

(Albert Van Siclen Pulling)

Stackpole Books

Published by
STACKPOLE BOOKS
Cameron and Kelker Streets
P.O. Box 1831
Harrisburg, PA 17105

First paperback edition, January 1989

Printed in the United States of America

10   9   8   7   6   5   4   3   2   1

Library of Congress Cataloging-in-Publication Data

Pulling, Pierre, 1891–
     Canoeing the Indian way : straight talk for modern paddlers from
the dean of American canoeists / Pierre Pulling (Albert Van Siclen
Pulling). — 1st pbk. ed.
          p.   cm.
     Reprint. Originally published: New York : McKay, © 1979.
     Includes index.
     ISBN 0-8117-2241-4 (pbk.)
     1. Canoes and canoeing.   2. Indians of North America — Boats.
I. Title.
     [GV783.P78 1989]
     797.1′22—dc19   88-19206

To the memory of my wife Dickie,
a gallant lady and a great canoeist

CONTENTS

Preface

This preface is so important that I trust you will not skip it.

Canoeing the Indian Way is the only book, to my rather certain knowledge, that is concerned with aboriginal paddling. That is, except for what I have previously written. Discounting various short articles of mine, I gave considerable attention to Indian canoeing in a book called *The Elements of Canoeing*, published by the Ann Arbor Press in 1933. A more comprehensive *Principles of Canoeing* was published by Macmillan in 1954. Both of these books are long out of print. *Canoeing the Indian Way*, with the permission of Macmillan, borrows from my *Principles* book.

Early in 1976, a little paperback that I wrote for Indians—*Indian Canoeing*—was copyrighted by Mon-

1

tana Indian Publication Fund and distributed by
Montana Reading Publications of Billings. I have
permission to quote from that little book, and its
editor, Hap Gilliland, has seen some aboriginal for-
eign canoeing that I have not. He has been most
helpful.

Though my earlier canoeing books acknowledged
much help, and this gratitude still holds, I have
needed little additional assistance for this book. Of
course, secretary Cherie Kremer translated my grotesque longhand. And editor Chet Fish was an
inspiration as well as a skilled technician. Artist Linda
Wolfe managed essential drawings. I'm grateful to
several photographers, especially Lloyd Furniss.
That is pretty much "it," except for considerable
mention of various people in the text.

Likewise, though my past canoe books included
bibliographies, this one does not. In writing it, I read
nothing essential except what I had written myself. I
learned aboriginal canoeing in 1914, and since then I
have read libraries on canoeing. But that reading,
though sometimes interesting, taught me little. And
very little of it touched on Indian paddling. I later
refer to a couple of books on canoes that are very
important. But one of the writers said he knew
nothing of Indian paddling, and there was nothing
in the other's writing suggesting that he used anything except power and ruddering to push his craft.

The basic arrangement of *Canoeing the Indian Way*
is that each chapter is rather separate. My hope is
that you can read any of them first. So a little
repetition is unavoidable.

I am a hunter and flycaster, and I wrote one

Pierre Pulling holds two of his favorite paddles as he stands in front of trailer that hauls two canoes. Beavertail paddle in his right hand is correct length for him to use in the bow. Slightly longer paddle in his left hand is best length for his stern paddling. Wrappings of twine protect the paddle shafts. Upper canoe is a 16-foot bark model made by the noted Henri Vaillancourt. Lower one is a fiberglass 18-footer from Herter. Pulling says that Targhee, the setter, is an excellent canoe dog but has not learned to paddle.

chapter, "Canoeing for the Sportsman and Woodsman," for myself and for readers with similar interests.

But I hope all camp, school, or club canoe instructors—though some will omit the part concerned with shooting and fishing—will grind through everything.

I have tried for brevity, hoping it is not conspicuous. The book must be compact, to go on canoe trips if you have not mastered everything.

Still, in spite of my effort to be brief, I include some incidents that many people have found interesting. A couple are downright flattering! I have learned aboriginal canoeing, and some aborigines have agreed. Not too common a situation.

All of my paddling techniques have been learned from Indians, though I admit much association with white guides and woodsmen in Quebec, Ontario, and New Brunswick. These people had learned just about as I had.

Though I borrowed the strokes, I had to name them myself.

In my first two books, I had to consider some stroke names and methods—totally "Paleface"—with which I disagreed. But those names and methods were so popular that I couldn't avoid giving them some attention. A vast number of people gave eloquent lip service to Indian canoeing. But they knew and cared nothing about Indian paddling, and in some instances (not all), violently opposed it.

As long ago as May 1914, I was dead sure that the aborigines knew how to paddle. Now there seems to be a tendency toward agreement with that opinion.

I have paid little attention to camp "war canoeing." War canoes are managed about the same as smaller ones. There is just more canoe. They need more judgment but are almost impossible to upset. Yet, in high waves they swamp easily.

I have also paid little attention to kayaks and double-blade paddles. Kayaks are usually handled well, and strokes are simple. A lone paddler with a double-blade paddle can buck a wind that is un-buckable with a single blade. I have used double blades considerably when working alone.

Finally, I have not considered canoe camping, except very casually. As I see it, camping is camping.

In canoe camping, the campers use canoes for transport, about like camping with a packstring. Good books are available on canoe camping. My writing is largely on aspects of canoeing that are neglected.

I believe it was the late Elbert Hubbard who wrote: "Never explain. Your friends need no explanations. Your enemies will not believe them." Really, I rarely do explain my opinions and never apologize. So any errors are all mine. But I will cheerfully defend them!

—*Pierre Pulling,*
Idaho State University
Pocatello, Idaho
March 1979

The Canoe Belongs

The canoe is the most interesting link that unites the past and future of the outdoors. It may be the only still-popular but truly aboriginal tool that we have inherited. It has a beauty and grace that continue to intrigue the artist, and yet it carries its master and his property with a competent mulish buoyancy.

The only transportation device that I can compare with the canoe is the changeless pack or saddle animal. Trade, romance, religion, adventure, and erudition all put halos on faithful beasts of burden and equally faithful canoes. A faithful donkey carried the young Christ into Egypt. Smashing ancestors of the Clydesdale and Shire bore knights into battle. Sleek Arabians made up Coronado's cavalry. Canoes, however, transported Jesuit missionaries to the four winds in eastern America. Canoes carried much of the local freight of an early civilization. Canoes sailed unbelievable distances in the South Seas. Canoes, in gondola form, are still the most romantic craft in the world's most artistic nation.

As other early tools give ground, the canoe and a few of its associates—such as the Eskimo kayak—increase in popularity. It is still the willing slave of the prospector, the hunter, the fisherman, the camper, and the adventurer. The hunter may pursue game or romance. The angler may be a fisher of salmon or of men. The prospector can be seeking gold or art. The paddling camper is often escaping from civilization's boredom, while the canoeing adventurer is perhaps reliving the days of the Fur Brigade over the largely unchanged waters of Canada.

Like the packstring, the canoe is as old as history and as young as tomorrow's sunrise. Its future is as certain as its present. The best canoes ever built are on the modern market, and nothing of such beauty, grace, and utility can ever grow old.

Still, as in the days of yore, the canoe demands a master. I repeat that it is mulish. Some people say "cranky." A horse or a dog may work through sheer devotion to any human, but a mule's handler must know more than a mule! A clumsy barge may slowly and safely transport gross baggage with a crude pilot. The canoe is docile only when managed with skill and judgment. Nothing inanimate is so human, though the small sailboat—including the sailing canoe—is comparable. Nobody can, like Hiawatha, guide his canoe solely by thought. But the elements of paddling are so simple that thought becomes action with no apparent time lapse.

Idaho canoeists Ted Pulling (stern) and Ernest Naftzger put a Vaillancourt bark canoe through its paces. The water hasn't frozen, but the air is very cold.

Complementary to the modern charm and fascinating background of the canoe is the fact that master canoeists are still around. Like master mariners in sail, they are rare, but canoeing is no lost art. There are canoeists both at home and abroad who can do anything with a canoe that anyone ever did. Furthermore, they can teach almost anyone excellent canoeing.

Though no older art is quite comparable to canoeing, it is true that excellent bows, Kentucky-type rifles, fine saddlery, and the best axes of all time are available today, as well as canoes and paddles. And there are still masters in the uses of all these old implements to tutor those who care.

I repeat that many of these time-honored arts are not lost. No more lost than the study of classical cultures. But nowadays you may be considered fairly well educated without studying ancient Greek. You can cook lunch without first splitting kindling. And sometimes you may travel by other means on waters that once demanded a canoe. In many instances, the canoe is still the most beautiful, the most logical, and the most efficient means of travel. At times it is still the only suitable craft for certain waters. And propelled by paddle.

Incidentally, the rather recent ecological and environmental interests have boosted canoeing. The canoe belongs!

And finally, consider energy. Not only is a canoe no polluter of air and water, but gasoline is not needed to push a paddle. It is true that the paddler may more heavily menace the food supply than he would if he remained less active, but you can't have everything.

So let's stop explaining and philosophizing and have at it.

1

How I Learned to Paddle

In May of 1914, I had been perhaps a week on my Quebec woods job. One evening, from headquarters camp, I went out alone to troll with a heavy handline on Lac Serpent.

As I came in, our only Indian in the 14-man outfit was on the beach. He was a young Abenikee named Isadore Meconse. Isadore was an amazing young man. I doubt if he could read a word in any language. But he could get along in English, spoke good-enough French, and was fluent in both the Algonquian and Iroquois languages. He also had an astounding sense of direction. Please do not refer to this as a "sixth" sense. There may be 15 senses or more. Senses of direction, balance, rhythm, and danger are almost as simple as the five senses commonly accepted. But some folks do not have them, just as few humans have more than a rudimentary sense of smell. But all this is the typical digression of an old professor. Let's get back to Isadore as he stood there on the lakeshore.

He helped me turn over the canoe and allowed as how I had a couple of big fish, which we cleaned for the cook and breakfast. Then Isadore casually remarked that maybe tomorrow evening, if I wished, he would show me how to paddle.

In Isadore's best English, this was not unduly complimentary, but I was aware that I just might be the crew's most ignorant canoeist. On the instant, I decided to become the best or certainly as good as the best.

I was in the same timber-cruising crew as Isadore for perhaps two months. Whenever we had a spare hour, I had him teach me paddling. He knew it all. But within a couple of years, I could explain as much paddling in an hour as I had learned from Isadore that summer. Though he lacked the experience of his elders (he was only 19 or 20), he had the rudiments of all the aboriginal canoeing that existed anywhere—from Quebec to the South Seas, through the African jungles, and around to Venice in Italy.

Perhaps I should again digress to emphasize that a gondolier *paddles* his romantic craft. Isadore could have stepped into any gondola on the Grand Canal and in short order made it sit up and beg. And after a summer of paddling lessons from Isadore, so could I.

In September just two years later, I was flattered. My employers "loaned" me, as a slightly glorified guide, to Dr. Samuel Upham of Claremont, New

Hampshire. The doctor was a member of the Triton Club on the Quebec and Lac St. John Railroad, north of the city of Quebec. He usually spent September there. Fishing was still good, flycasting as good as it was at any time of the year. And shooting started September 1.

Dr. Upham—fiftyish and a big, strong man—had not been very well. His heart misbehaved some, and he had to quit smoking. The Triton Club guides were pretty much Hurons, who spoke little or no English. They all had acceptable French, which Dr. Upham did not. I spoke and understood enough French to get along. Mrs. Upham violently opposed the doctor's going out with guides who could not talk to him at all. Hence the deal with me.

When Dr. Upham and I stopped at the Triton Club siding, the doctor's old head guide, Eugene, was waiting with a big canoe. Of course the doctor and I were in our "store" clothes. I helped get our duffle out of the baggage car and loaded into the canoe. Then, when everything was ready, I made a thoughtless mistake. I was back at the stern, so I picked up a paddle and got in. My action was impulsive. I had been steering a canoe all summer. But I was immediately aware of my blunder and started to get out. Eugene began to sputter in at least two languages, maybe three.

But Dr. Upham roared at Eugene to get into the bow and for me to stay where I was. So we took off for the couple of miles on a crooked creek to the clubhouse.

The canoe was rather heavily loaded, and the balance was less than perfect. It was not easy to manage. Eugene looked back occasionally, perhaps to see if I was still there. Anyway we made it without comment or incident.

During the evening, I found that Eugene, though a competent canoeist in all respects, was preferably a right-handed bow paddler and was perhaps 15 pounds lighter than I. Bow or stern, I am at my best on the left. Of course the guide is the canoe captain and usually the steersman, unless he chooses otherwise.

Next morning in my voyageur's clothes, I helped load the canoe. Then I got into the bow, where I belonged. We crossed a lake, a portage, another lake, and the second portage. Eugene lugged the canoe. The cargo load was big, so we each came back for a second pack. Eugene found that I could lug as much as he could. Dr. Upham carried his rifle, flyrod, camera, binoculars, and such minor gear—not over 30 pounds and one trip.

Anyway, at the end of the second portage, Eugene loaded the canoe a bit differently, grinned, pointed me to the rear, and said, "Now Eugene go front."

Dr. Upham smiled and said, "Well, Pierre, you have qualified with a good woods professional."

I was proud enough. Still am.

Then there was another bit of Indian flattery about a decade later, possibly 1927. I was teaching then and working summers for organized camps. That summer, I was at the Highland Nature Camps on Sebago Lake in Maine. We were on a mid-August trip up above the Rangely Lakes on the Magalloway River, the last evening before turning for home camp. We had pitched camp relatively early. It was after supper and still broad daylight when an Indian drifted into camp. He introduced himself as Joe Buckshot, an Old Town, who was cutting pulpwood a scant ¼ mile from our meadow camp. My girls had a plate of cookies and a cup of tea for him in a trice.

Joe spoke fair-enough English. Better French. Probably all of my campers were private-school students and had studied French. The jabbering was terrific!

Suddenly Joe asked if our girls were Indians. They weren't, but they had suitable Indian coloring. They had taken great pains to get an even tan.

Our discussion was still going on when one of my stern paddlers shoved her canoe into the river and paddled across a bay for a load of driftwood. She was a tall, stunning girl named Ruth London. Ruth was from Boston and was scheduled to enter Smith in the fall. Joe looked in wonder and said, *"That* girl is an Indian. No white person could paddle like that."

I explained that I had taught her, and that I was Indian-trained. Abenikee, Montagnais, Huron, and Milicete. I had yet to work with Ojibways, Crees, and Eskimos. Joe was as amused as I was flattered. But he was still unconvinced. To him, Ruth was an Indian. Anyway, Joe Buckshot knew a good paddler when he saw one in action.

In the summer of 1928, my wife and I were working for the brother-and-sister camps Ossippee an Pine Knoll in New Hampshire. My time was split; but my wife was the senior counselor at Pine Knoll, and usually I was there on weekends.

Mrs. Bucher, Pine Knoll's director, was elderly and not very strong. She leaned heavily on Assistant

Director Ray Morrill. I had known Ray for a dozen years, and I appreciated his ability. He was a fine canoeist, which Mrs. Bucher was not.

Still Mrs. Bucher had a private canoe. It had been an expensive Old Town and had metal sponsons. No one except Mrs. Bucher used it—someone else paddling—and I doubt if she rode in it four times a season.

Perhaps I should note here how awful and useless sponsons are. I have not seen any in years, nor have I seen them advertised. But I have a slick sporting magazine on my desk that advertises detachable pontoons. I don't like that idea any better.

Sponsons were "floats" built out on both sides of the canoe. They were formed of either hollow metal or built-up layers of cork. Their purpose was supposedly to make the canoe unsinkable. A proper canoe already is unsinkable unless it's loaded with kitchen stoves or many cases of beer. Anyway, sponsons appealed to people who were timid, ignorant, or both.

This craft of Mrs. Bucher's was so heavy that no one would haul it out and put it on the canoe racks. Or maybe it was Mrs. Bucher's choice to have it carefully tethered just off the dock. A couple of light blocks and a piece of cotton clothesline made it easy to haul in. There it sat, week after week, soaking up water. It was bailed out regularly, but it became badly waterlogged.

One Saturday night we had a furious thunderstorm. And when the before-breakfast swimmers went for their quick dips, that old sponson canoe had disappeared. Some miscreant had slipped in under cover of the storm and stolen it.

Though Mrs. Bucher had rarely used this ancient tub, she was devoted to it. Its disappearance made her very upset. She called the county sheriff and the state police. The uproar was intense.

Ray Morrill and I discussed the situation over breakfast. I have long had minor law-enforcement responsibility. Right now, for instance, I am a Bannock County Deputy Sheriff and an Idaho State ex-officio conservation officer. Everyone knows that much crime solving is managed by legwork and common sense.

The canoe was gone, but why? It was the worst canoe in camp and the hardest to get at. No one would choose it except to plague its owner, and she had no bitter enemies. Besides, possible pranksters had been in bed, with no interest in downpour prowling. So the canoe had not been stolen at all. It had sunk: the unsinkable sponson.

The small lake was totally calm the morning after the storm and only slightly roiled. We could see the canoe lying on its side in maybe 8 feet of water. As we learned, one sponson had a small hole. Water had so lowered the craft that the lake could seep in and fill the sponson. The other sponson could not quite keep the waterlogged canoe afloat. Ray dived for the broken tethering line. The canoe needed less than a 10-pound pull to drag it to the surface.

We drained the hull and also drained and patched the sponson. We again tethered the canoe. For all I know, it may still be there. My wife and I left New England that fall.

2

Canoeing Equipment

.

Canoes

You can learn to paddle in practically any sort of canoe. But you should observe a few principles when you try to get experience and develop judgment. Canoes are made of various materials and in various sizes, just as there are a lot of saddle trees, a number of axe patterns, and a good many rifle calibers. The manufacturers try to give customers what they want. Not that the customers always know what they *should* want.

Other things being equal, I suggest that you get the bigger canoe if you are in doubt. Right now, for general use, my favorite canoe is the standard-weight aluminum 18-foot job made by Grumman of Marathon, New York. (I own no Grumman stock!) Mine is about 36 inches wide amidships and about 13 inches deep. It has a shoe keel. The front seat is dipped, but it *should* be flush with the gunwales so that a paddler can kneel and get big feet under the seat comfortably. Aluminum canoes are pressed in two pieces and must have some sort of a keel to rivet them together. Grumman charges extra for a sensible shoe keel.

Long ago, some conservatives decided that a deep keel made a canoe "safer." Perhaps such a keel does make a canoe handle easier for people who don't know how to paddle (the vast majority), so I must not unduly criticize the manufacturers. And a standard deep keel is no disadvantage in any lake. But this deep keel simply makes the canoe harder to manage in a current and is downright dangerous in real rapids. A deep keel is of no advantage anywhere to a real canoeist.

I am not writing for goofers who want to remain goofers, so thumbs down on deep keels. The smaller shoe keel is no disadvantage and does provide some protection. Incidentally, no aboriginal canoe maker that I know about ever put a keel on a canoe. They follow a similar attitude in omitting seats.

Another of my canoes is an 18-foot plastic job from Herter, Rt. 2, Mitchell, South Dakota 57301. (Herter was formerly in Waseca, Minnesota.) It is keelless. Herter's keelless canoes cost less than one they sell with a keel. I think their keel job is simply ghastly! These Herter canoes are heavy but very seaworthy, and the seats are placed properly. But mine, when I got it, had the floats under the seats. The feet of a paddler couldn't be tucked under the scats.

I also have a standard 15-foot aluminum Grumman, primarily for working alone. It will slide into the bed of my pickup truck. I use this small one because nowadays I can't put the 18-foot canoe on top of the truck alone the way I used to. The heavy Herter requires two canoeists to load it onto a truck, but it handles fine otherwise.

Canoes of metal and fiberglass vastly outsell cedar-and-canvas models. I do not recall seeing an aluminum canoe until about 1949, and fiberglass a bit later. But really, I like cedar-and-canvas canoes better. Canoes made of cedar and canvas need considerable care, especially shelter from the elements. An aluminum canoe can lie out in the weather for perhaps half a century and suffer practically no harm.

I still have what is left of a canvas canoe that I got in 1937 from the Canadian Canoe Company of Peterboro, Ontario. I believe Canadian is now merged with the Chestnut Canoe Company of Fredericton, New Brunswick. My hunch is that the Canadian canoe builders know how to paddle, though many of the builders in the United States presumably do not. There was an exception: the E.M. White Canoe Company of Old Town, Maine, made really good cedar-and-canvas canoes. There were maybe three Old Town canoe makers, but White was by far the best by my standards. If I were buying a canvas canoe now, I would check with Chestnut or the Old Town Canoe Company of Old Town, Maine.

This old cedar-and-canvas canoe of mine is called the Prospector model. Though a bit slow, it is very useful. It's only 16 feet long, but 36 inches wide in the center and 14 inches deep. It is keelless. It has 850 pounds of capacity with 4 inches of freeboard. That's not enough freeboard in waves, but I have loaded this little canoe with half a ton for short distances in good water. An 18-foot Prospector will manage 1,000 pounds in any reasonable water.

My old canoe has been re-covered twice, and I have wondered if it rates still another skin. Perhaps not, as it was badly abused by some well-meaning but untutored college boys. This may be the place to note that untrained canoeists can be unconsciously careless. You should know well those people to whom you lend a canoe. Not too bad a philosophy about loaning anything.

At one time "war" canoes were very popular in organized camps. There were smallish 25-foot canoes and the big ones 35 or 36 feet long. All of those I have seen were cedar and canvas, and they rate very careful storage to keep them from getting "hogged," which is a term for a bent bottom. When turned upside down on shore or under a shed (and they should be kept under cover), they should be supported in three places.

If you are to use war canoes at all, I suggest the big ones. And keels are all right because these canoes aren't used in crooked streams.

Really long and relatively shallow canoes—though they're great fun, fast, and hard to fall out of—are easily swamped by short waves and demand the judgment of a canoeist. Usually 20-foot guide models are big enough. And Grumman has rigged a big 20-foot aluminum canoe like a war canoe (you kneel or sit on wide thwarts). It will manage maybe eight young campers and is relatively foolproof. Any good 20-foot canoe, on trips, will manage four campers and their equipment.

Before leaving the discussion of cedar-and-canvas canoes, I should note that one reason I like them is that they follow the spirit of Indian construction. The filled canvas takes the place of the Indian's bark. There is an added interest in bark canoes as I write. There is no reason for me to dwell on them here as Bulletin 230 of the Smithsonian Institution in Washington covers them beautifully. This bulletin is called "The Bark Canoes and Skin Boats of North America." Any canoe coach or advanced canoeist should study it. The Superintendent of Documents, Washington, sells it.

There are a very few bark-canoe builders at work now. Henri Vaillancourt of Greenville, New Hampshire, is one of them. Idaho State University (Pocatello), where I am a retired professor, has one of his canoes. It is largely an Abenikee type (you may want to spell it "Abnaki") with a Montagnais touch. It is 16 feet long and tippy for beginners but tough and seaworthy for its dimensions.

I had an Abenikee canoe myself for many years. It was covered by one piece of bark and was about 14 feet long. I saw one 16½-foot canoe made from a single piece of bark. It was from a mighty birch. Mr. Vaillancourt is not technically trained in anthropology, but he is very accurate. Of course, he is a student of that Smithsonian bulletin. Like the natives, he uses few tools. The ribs and planking of his canoes are hand-split from arborvitae logs. I will consider a few more details on aboriginal manufacturing in the next chapter.

Paddles

Anthropological reports show paddles that seem to be grotesque and outlandish. If you have access to a big library, look at *Souvenirs de Marine* by the late Captain Paris of the French Navy. It covers world canoes and paddles more completely than anything else I have seen. The only copy I recall studying is in the John Crerar Library in Chicago.

You should especially note that, even though paddles as well as canoes vary a lot, all aboriginals use paddles pretty much identically. And the Venetian gondolier paddles with an oar. He uses it like a paddle, but it is awkward for me not to have a flat knob at the top of a paddle.

I will largely consider North American Indian paddle types and materials. You will do fine if you follow these views. Later you may like something else better. Some advertised paddles I dislike, mainly because I consider their blades too wide.

Paddles should usually have blades about 6 inches wide. If you paddle with them long enough, they will be worn or sanded narrower. If a blade is only 5 inches wide, it will be no handicap to you. I have an old Cree paddle that's only 3 inches wide and has a very long blade, so there is plenty of water resistance.

Three paddles from the collection of Hap Gilliland, expert in aboriginal canoeing. The one at left is a common North American shape. Center paddle, hanging upside down, is from the Mikeritari Indians in South America. At right: paddle used by the Tlingit Indians of Alaska. Though canoe paddles vary considerably in shape from one culture to another, methods of paddling remain essentially constant among aboriginal peoples.

For his own use, Pierre Pulling favors a paddle of conventional design, one that provides him with a flat knob at the top of the shaft.

Maybe the Crees made them narrow because the available black spruces took a couple of centuries to grow 3 inches in diameter. A canoeist uses what he must.

For steering an ordinary canoe, I like a paddle 66 inches long. Sixty-three inches, for bow. I usually kneel. I'm 69 inches tall, so the paddles are 3 inches and 6 inches shorter than I am. Not a bad set of dimensions. For a freight canoe, where you may well sit a lot and be higher, paddles 3 inches longer are, in my experience, better.

I like a square-tip paddle better than a beaver tail. Actually, the paddle's shape, if it's not too wide, makes little difference in use. I use what is available without appreciable worry. If a blade is too wide, I can fix it with my good jackknife.

For lake paddling, spruce is just about universal. My pet is glued in three pieces. That is, the shaft is. The maker had only one-inch stock. Good glue holds wood rigidly indeed, especially if the wood is occasionally spar-varnished. At least once a season, any paddle should be sanded with No. 0 sandpaper, wiped clean, and then lightly varnished. The tip, if it's a bit "broomed," should be thoroughly dried and then really soaked with varnish.

Hardwood paddles are usually made of sugar maple or white ash. Black cherry *(Prunus serotina)* may be even better. These hardwoods are heavier than spruce, but paddles made of them can be slimmer. The paddle edges can be sharper and will cut the water better. A slim paddle throat (lower grip) is important for any paddler with small hands. My hands are big, so a thick grip is no problem.

The photos in this book show my paddles wrapped with twine. A ball I have is labeled "Cotton Seine Twine." It is 40-pound-test. It's no trick to wrap the paddle shaft. The technique is about the same as the one used in whipping rope ends. Then the paddle wrapping should be soaked with spar varnish or, possibly better, with plastic glass. If the wrapping gets at all frayed by gunwale friction, take it off and rewrap. Twine is cheaper than paddles and may prevent a break in the middle of bad rapids or in some other dangerous or awkward situation. The same twine is recommended if you need a "sideline" to connect the shaft to the canoe in anticipation of possible upsetting.

I also recommend ¼-inch cotton or nylon rope for hang-on loops on each thwart. I have never needed either, as I never upset. But I might.

Unless your knees are extra tough, you need a kneeling cushion. A proper kneeling cushion is long enough for you to kneel with your knees comfortably apart. Or you can strap on rubber knee pads. They are made for garden weeders and other people who spend a lot of time on their knees. Foam rubber is fine kneeling-cushion material, but it won't float unless it's enclosed in a waterproof wrapping.

My hands are depigmented, and I am a slave to gloves. I like Indian-tanned deerskin gloves the best. In cold weather I wear heavy deerskin chopper's mittens with warm wool liners. I coat the mittens with neat's-foot oil or any good leather grease. Your lower hand may get wet, so the wool liner is important. I have dry gloves to slip on for shooting or for fly-casting during cold weather.

For portaging, there are commercial yokes that can be strapped to the canoe, and all sorts of paddle-yoke devices are available. I like a yoke that's built in and replaces the middle thwart. I also like to have a tump-line attached. You do not mislay a yoke if it is bolted in, nor do you hunt for a headline that's attached.

I made the yoke for my old Prospector model from a slab of basswood. Light "soft hardwood" such as basswood or tulip poplar (whitewood) are fine and easy to work. I once made a yoke of black ash, and it worked as well. The wood was a bit heavier, but you can make the yoke slimmer. I have seen yokes made of Philippine "mahogany."

It is scarcely worthwhile to specify yoke dimensions. I cut-and-try on my own shoulders, but all men who have used my yoke like it. I am rather bull-necked, perhaps from tumpline packing. A 16½-inch shirt neck feels better if it is not buttoned.

Few women can lug an ordinary canoe without undue punishment. With all due respect to women's lib, I believe that women had best get a man for the heavy portaging.

3

Some Canoeing Details

In Chapter 2, I referred to the Smithsonian's Bulletin 230, "The Bark Canoes and Skin Boats of North America." Many canoeing students will choose it for historical study. Bark-canoe maker Henri Vaillancourt of Greenville, New Hampshire, leaned on it heavily. So did John McPhee in his book *Survival of the Bark Canoe* (Farrar, Straus & Giroux). The book *How to Build an Indian Canoe,* published by David McKay, is a George Fichter adaptation of the bulletin.

But if you do not care for research elsewhere, let me recount a bit of rather ancient history here.

I continue to be interested in canvas-covered canoes for two reasons: 1) they are quiet, and 2) they are sentimentally parallel to the aboriginal's bark craft, the canvas taking the place of the bark.

Canoe-maker Vaillancourt, who is quite a competent anthropologist within this specialty, and writer McPhee may be oversanguine about early bark-canoe building. I am inclined to doubt that Indians built their really beautiful birch-bark boats until they got some "Paleface" tools. Bark canoes—real beauties—were made with no tools except an axe, a crooked knife, and perhaps awls or a brace and bit. The Indians made bone awls. Mr. Vaillancourt uses only these tools now, with the addition of a froe—a tool for more-precise splitting than is possible with an axe. A froe is a horizontal steel blade with a vertical wood handle. The blade is struck by a maul that may well be a wooden club.

That was a simple list of tools, but the bark-canoe artist had to have them. Certainly he had to have the axe and crooked knife. They were steel. Aboriginal Indians, so far as I can find out, were totally Stone Age before the earliest European explorers got here. I'm aware that there were some very primitive bark and skin boats long before European tools were available.

Far back in history, dugout canoes, or pirogues, were made by burning and scraping. In 1920, I saw good ones made new with few tools in New Brunswick. The trees were usually aspen or "cedar" *(Thuja occidentalis),* which is commonly called arborvitae or "white" cedar. The largest northeastern dugouts presumably were of white pine, but their makers said white pine was inclined to be warpy. I never saw one. And I never saw a canoe made of tulip poplar *(Liriodendron tulipifera* of the Magnolia family). But tulip poplar—or whitewood—may have been the best dugout timber in the East and Middle South.

The giant "war canoe" dugouts of the Northwest were made from "western red cedar" *(Thuja plicata).* Lewis and Clark's expedition made "cedar" dugouts to go down to salt water on the site of what is now Orofino, Idaho. Some of these dugouts were very big. One is in the American Museum of Natural History in New York City. It could float a small village.

As far back as 1931, when I was writing my first canoe book in Ann Arbor, Michigan, I was privileged to consult Dr. W.B. Hinsdale. Dr. Hinsdale was considered the leading Indian anthropologist of the Great Lakes region. He did not believe the Indians had made really good bark canoes until they got some simple white-man's tools early in the 1500s. I accept his opinion. Of course, Stone Age bark boats had existed earlier, but they must have been crude. If anyone believes the real beauties were made earlier, I must differ and ask for proof.

There was considerable variation in the length and design of bark canoes. My guide friend, the late Lloyd Melville, used one as short as 10 feet. I owned one of Abenikee design that was exactly 13 feet 8 inches long and was made of one piece of bark. And then there was that Abenikee job 16½ feet long made from the bark of a single tree.

Though designs differed, the construction was practically identical. The ribs were made of split arborvitae. So was the planking that was shoved between the ribs and bark but not nailed. The bark shrinkage made everything tight. Gunwales were either arborvitae or spruce. Thwarts might be any easily workable hardwood, usually white birch or black ash. The bark was stitched with roots of black spruce, and the seams were waterproofed with pine or spruce pitch into which a little tallow was mixed for flexibility.

The largest bark canoe of which I can find an authentic record was described in the recollections of Lieutenant Landman of the British Army. He wrote about his experiences as commander of Fort St. Joseph in 1798. I copy his description exactly as it was quoted in the *Sault Daily Star* 130 years later:

> These canoes were exceedingly strong and capacious, they were about thirty-six feet in length, by six wide, near the middle; and although the birch bark which formed thin external coating over their ribs of white cedar, and their longitudinal laths of the same woods, appeared to compose but a flimsy vessel, yet they usually carried a weight of five tons. It may be well to state that the cargo was very carefully stowed, in order to relieve any unequal pressure, which would have been fatal to such a vessel. Four poles, three to four inches in diameter at the thickest ends, denominated by the Canadians, grand perch, and nearly as long as the canoe, were laid side by side in the middle of the bottom of the canoe. On these poles the cargo was carefully arranged, so that all the weight rested on them. . . . Every package was made up to the weight of ninety pounds, and none heavier.

The five tons included the provision for ten men, sufficient to support them during about twenty to twenty-two days. Each canoe was provided with a mast and lug sail, and also each man had a ten foot setting pole, of good ash, and shod with an iron ferrule at each end, for assisting the men towing with a strong line ascending the rapids. The paddles were supplied by the canoe men, each bringing also his own. Each canoe had a camp kettle, provided by the owners, as, also, a few Hambro lines, a bundle of wataps, roots of the pine tree, for stitching up any seam that might burst, a parcel of gum of a resinous nature, for paying over the seams when leaky, a piece of birch bark for repairs, hatchet, crooked knife, and a few more indispensable articles.

The crew consisted of a guide, a steersman, and eight common paddlers, but all worked alike. The guide was paid as much as four ordinary men, and the steersman half as much. Sixteen to twenty pounds was about the wages of a good guide.

The "wataps" were presumably spruce roots rather than pine. The length of time the crew worked for those wages is obscure, but it was probably a month. Twenty pounds was about $100 in 1798 and probably top pay for a guide. This would imply peak wages of $50 a month for a steersman and $25 for a paddler and packer.

Times did not change too much in the next hundred years or so. I started at $35 a month as a green timber cruiser and canoe hand in May of 1914.

Lieutenant Landman left Montreal on May 12, 1798, in a freight canoe of the type described. He went up the Ottawa, crossed to Lake Nipissing, then down the French River to Georgian Bay in Lake Huron. After getting to the big water, he went up the North Channel to St. Joseph Island.

I have traveled by canoe over some of this route and have examined what is left of Fort St. Joseph. I have come to the conclusion that Lieutenant Landman was a conscientious and reasonably observant reporter.

These very large canoes were evidently made by the Ojibways. The big canoes could have been made under the influence of Athapascan-Cree culture, and we know that the Crees were somewhat influenced by the Eskimos. In any event, we will leave much of the rest of canoe history to the historians.

Just a few words now on other types of canoes or construction.

The kayak is Eskimo and originally was skin-covered. Eskimo umiaks were big, skin-covered craft propelled by single-blade paddles, or sometimes sailed.

Some all-wood canoes were popular at one time. I saw painted basswood canoes with elm frames, and racing canoes made of "cigar-box cedar" *(Cedrela odorate)*. And there were molded-veneer canoes. As smooth inside as out. Probably a layer of western arborvitae between two layers of yellow birch, not the paper birch that furnished canoe bark.

Anyway, we might as well, as a general rule, forget everything except aluminum and fiberglass where new canoes are concerned. A cedar-and-canvas canoe should be treasured. And, of course, if you can get a bark job, that rates tender and loving care.

Finally, I must mention the bark-covered canoes with down-tipped ends made by the Kootenai Indians in North Idaho and into Canada. It amazes me that identically designed canoes have been made on the Amur River in Asia.

I have never seen a Kootenai canoe, but the late Dr. Laurence A. Gale, a native of Idaho's Boundary County, had used them. Apparently the bark was elm. But I saw two similar canoes from Asia in a Chicago museum, and they were covered with birch bark that closely resembled our native canoe bark.

There is some very interesting speculation about travel by raft—even canoe—across the Pacific, both north and south. I would cheerfully paddle the Bering Straits myself if there was no Iron Curtain. Perhaps some Amur River culture wandered to the Kootenai and stuck. In any event, I'm satisfied enough that our Eskimos were Asiatic Mongols and relative newcomers to America. And there seems little doubt that the ancestors of North American Indians were also Asiatic.

4

Canoeing Safety

Some people have a peculiar fear of canoes. I am not a good enough psychologist to explain it. This fear is partially bred by ignorance—like some people's fear of guns. Water—like fire—is a magnificent servant but a cruel master.

My late father was afraid of canoes even though he had never been in one. He was relatively well informed but sadly arbitrary. He did not understand why I refused to be drowned. How is it that American Indians and other aborigines paddled all their lives in far greater safety than today's motorist?

Aboriginals, and all woods professionals who depended on canoes, have followed a somewhat elaborate unwritten safety code. I have observed five distinct elements:

1.   They were good canoeists. They could paddle.

2.   They had good judgment. Or before they acquired the experience that usually develops judgment, they depended on someone who had it.

3.   As good canoeists with good judgment, they rarely allowed themselves to get into a dangerous situation.

4.   If, in spite of precautions, a dangerous situation developed, they usually had the skill to paddle out of it.

5.   If the worst came to the worst and they were wrecked or swamped, they did *not* swim; they hung on to the canoe until their feet were on bottom and they could walk ashore.

In anticipation of possible wrecking or swamping, precautions were taken to hang on to the canoe. I have paddled thousands of miles with the middle of my paddle shaft connected to a thwart by maybe six feet of sideline, codline, or some other strong cord. In case of swamping, you'd hang on to the paddle instinctively, I hope. You will need the paddle later. You are towed by the paddle until you can get a death grip on the canoe. And I mean a *death* grip. There are numerous records of corpses hanging on after they have died from exposure.

The canoeist's nightmare is to be swamped and lose the canoe. In really cold water, that tragedy is about as grim as a horseman's being thrown and having one foot caught in a stirrup.

Furthermore, you should have cotton rope loops, or looped bandana handkerchiefs, tied to each side of each thwart to facilitate hanging on. I have never needed them, but they have added to my feeling of safety when situations looked dangerous. If the situation looks at all sticky, the canoe should not be loaded heavily. Under ideal conditions, I have transported a kitchen stove in a canoe a couple of times, and you can bet that I was very cautious.

For upwards of a half century, the accepted U.S. canoeing authorities considered swimming to be the safety art for canoeists. Of course I agree that everyone should be able to swim. My aboriginal-canoeing associates and I don't quarrel with the accepted swimming and life saving techniques if they are applied to swimming and falling-in-from-the-bank situations. But I do quarrel with a philosophy that emphasizes teaching green canoeists to fall out and what to do when they fall out.

Young people tend to do what they are taught. Beginning in 1915, I have had extensive observation of organized camps that use canoes. I worked for organized camps, as a canoe coach, the seasons of 1922-1933 inclusive. The seasons of 1934-1940, my wife was canoe coach in an organized camp, and I visited and helped most weekends.

Though I kept no exact statistics during this extensive camp experience, some figures were obvious. Before I (we) worked for those camps, upsets and swim-outs were common. When we moved on to another camp, the upsets came back.

To the best of my memory, I recall only four upsets while my wife and I were coaching camp canoeing.

• One girl, who had had no instruction, took a canoe out without permission on a windy, rainy day. She upset not 50 feet from the dock.

• A crew of girls, on a trip, tangled with a treetop that was nearly across the Magalloway River. Four canoes steered past it properly. The fifth one did not.

• Then, also on trips, we had *two* crews of boys upset. In both instances they were playing a big fish. One of these crews managed to retrieve everything, including the fish. The other lost some expensive tackle and the fish.

There just may have been other foolish accidents in some 19 seasons. In all but the one case, the canoeists were good. There was never any danger of drowning. In one situation tackle was lost. In another, wet camping gear.

During all this camp canoeing, I was embarrassed by what were then called "canoe tests."

These tests were practically all swimming tests. The camp kids took canoes out, upset them, towed them ashore, and this-and-that. All in the water. They were taught to upset, and they did it effectively. The sad part was that if a camper caught cold, the camp nurse ruled that he or she could not do any other swimming. And (I was always in North Woods situations) there were periods of cold, rainy weather when these tests were—wisely enough—prohibited because of weather conditions. The basic problem was that the campers, as canoeists, were *taught* to upset. So occasionally they did.

(Please note that these camp directors were ethically bound to follow the canoe-test rules.)

I always managed to get around these rules one

way or another. The simplest was in a camp where my wife and I worked 1925 through 1927. The camp had a number of double-end canvas-covered rowboats. They were of canoe construction and as good as canoes for preliminary instruction. Because they were classified as boats, they were deemed safe. So I used them. The 35-foot war canoes were canoes, and the authorities considered them not safe. Another camp had a paddling barge we could use. And so on.

So our campers learned to paddle better than *any* other campers. Superlatives are always questionable, but here I use one without any doubts. We got results in spite of a well-meant safety regulation. The regulations, I found out, were largely the result of ignorance about effective canoeing.

There were a number of die-hards. The camp at which I worked in 1922 had three directors. One was the water authority for what was then the Camp Directors Association. He was largely responsible for those "canoe tests." We had some mean weather that summer and an epidemic of colds. He and I maintained the amenities, but we really tangled. He maintained that canoes upset and that when they did, the problem was *swimming*. I claimed that properly coached campers did not upset and that even if they did, the procedure was to hang on. Camp canoeists were operating not over 100 yards from the dock, so rescue would be easy if there was an upset. Of course we had no upsets all season, except those planned in connection with the "tests." And we took the most difficult canoe trips that the camp, or perhaps any other, had ever attempted.

Eventually this "authority" (he never learned to paddle well, or even tried to learn) agreed that I could coach canoeists to *not* upset. He and I got on fine for the remaining six years I worked for New England camps. An intelligent but stubborn chap, he lost a wee bit of prestige when he changed his views.

I must insist that you remember those five aboriginal safety rules—especially the last one, which suggests that *you must not depend very much on swimming*. And note that young people do pretty much what they are trained to do. So I object to training them to upset. Upsetting is no laughing matter in the North, where my canoeing has largely been done. Sometimes the water is dangerously cold during cloudy, windy weather, even in midsummer.

During the summers of 1961-64, I was Ranger on Yellowstone Park's rather remote Shoshone Lake. All of our patrol was by canoe. Motorboats were legally prohibited on both Shoshone and its outlet. There were many hiking parties on the trails, and many canoes got in there. Usually they were badly paddled.

The doctors told us that the average active life of a person in the water, in either Yellowstone Lake or Shoshone Lake, was 20 minutes if the weather was cloudy or windy. At that elevation (almost 8,000 feet), winds and clouds were common. At such times, very deep, cold water was whipped to the surface. Fortunately there were no upsets during four seasons. I told the campers they could drown out of my territory if they wanted to but that I did not care to fish for corpses and make out death reports.

I have been told that in the North sea, most people were helpless after 9 minutes. And I believe that is about what holds anywhere in deep water for really northern canoeists.

In the summer of 1937, I helped some polar-bear hunters on the east coast of James Bay. We continued into Hudson Bay to some extent. It was an all-around exploring trip. The big party included three women, one of whom was Jane Carrott, a Bennington student. Our general transport was a 45-foot auxiliary schooner. When we were at anchor, Jane usually took a brief swim every day. She would dive off the deck, swim furiously maybe 25 yards and back. Then we dragged her up onto the deck. That 50 yards was about all she could manage in water so cold.

While we were anchored off the Fort George ("Big") River, hundreds of Crees and many canoes were on shore when Jane took her swim. Our Norwegian skipper, the late Jack Palmquist, spoke Cree. He told us these Indians had never before seen a human being swim. Yet they were good canoeists. They paddled and sailed long distances. They studied the weather and learned when to go ashore and how long to stay there. In keeping with the unwritten code, they either developed judgment or leaned on someone who had it. I will not say there were no casualties. All seas are cruel. But such incidents were rare.

With or without canoe experience, you can always find a few philosophies to keep in mind. I often quote to green canoeists the last stanza of Henry Drummond's "Wreck of the Julie Plant":

> Now all good woodscow sailor man
> Tak warning by dat storm;
> Go an marry one nice French gal
> An leeve on wan beeg farm;
> De win she blow lak hurricane,
> An spose she blow some more?
> You can't get drown on Lac San Pierre,
> So long you stay on shore.

And the late famous writer Robert Ruark, who was a world traveler, sometimes changed flights after meeting the pilot. If the weather was questionable or the flight transoceanic, he liked a pilot who was past 50. He claimed that there were old pilots and bold pilots but that the bold ones were never old.

The same goes for canoeists. And I will be 87 before this book gets into print. Of course I have taken calculated risks. All of my field work via canoe, saddle, truck, or foot has been a bit hazardous. Maybe I have had luck. Some luck never hurt anyone. But most of the risks were calculated. A canoeist may paddle a lifetime with no appreciable accidents.

The oldtime voyageurs paddled Lake Superior and everything to the northwest, and they usually got to where they were going. But they knew when to get on shore and boil tea. I have paddled Superior's north shore some myself, and we boiled for more hours than we paddled.

These professionals did not always make it. I have seen some Indian graves at the bottoms of Canadian rapids. Those paddlers were bold. Or drunk. Or calculated badly. Canoe travel in such waters deserves a respectful approach.

The aborigines, of course, never heard of a life preserver (or personal flotation device, as some people now call them). And since any suitable canoe, even when swamped, will float its crew longer than they're likely to live, life jackets are a topic that you may surmise should get little attention in this book. True, except that some states have laws on the subject.

My own Idaho has a law that requires small-boat travelers to wear life preservers of a type approved by the Coast Guard. The enforcement agency, though, is the Idaho Fish and Game Department. An agent told me recently that they enforce the law only for motorboats. I have a good life jacket. Sometimes I carry it in a canoe, but I very rarely wear it.

The canoeists who make a sport of running white water will routinely wear life jackets. Upsets are common in that activity. An official flotation device, whether legally demanded or not, might make a practitioner of that art happier. The cost of a good life jacket is nominal, and it will last for years if you give it good care.

5

Paddling Methods

Since a good canoeist must first be a good paddler, the right strokes are of major importance.

You can learn to paddle from written instructions and from illustrations. But this way of learning demands meticulous attention. Remember Kipling's doctrine in *The Jungle Book?*

> For the head and the horn of the Law
> And the hoof and the hump is OBEY!

I am sticking to aboriginal strokes. The North American Indians knew how to paddle. Some alleged "authorities" doubted it in the too-recent past, but now there seems to be a swing back toward the Indian way. If you believe that the Indians (and natives worldwide) were wrong, you have already read too far in this book.

Please keep in mind that I report to you the methods exactly as they were taught to me. Yet neither the Indians I worked with nor the Canadian guides had any generally accepted names for these strokes. My Indian friends knew some English, and I knew a little French. I knew only a few words— mostly nouns—in their native languages. So I will not vouch for the stroke names. But the strokes themselves are authentic.

There are only four really basic strokes, and they should be learned and taught in the following order.

1. *Forward Stroke.* It shoves the canoe ahead. Done straight-away, it turns the canoe bow slightly away from the paddling side.

2. *Backing Stroke.* It backs the canoe. And it tends to swing the bow toward the paddling side.

3. *Draw Stroke.* This draws the canoe toward the paddle.

4. *Push-over Stroke.* This levers the canoe away from the paddle.

These are all the basic directions I can recognize. Something like north, south, east, and west.

Still, these four cardinal strokes do not make your canoe travel reasonably straight, and they don't manage all the turns. So three more strokes are required:

5. *Stern Steering Stroke.* This is a combination of the Forward Stroke and the Push-over Stroke. The Push-over element straightens the canoe as it moves ahead.

6. *Sweep.* A sort of combination of a Forward Stroke and a Draw Stroke. It turns the canoe away from your paddling side faster than does a plain

Forward Stroke. Practice will show that the Sweep has a contradictory effect if swept through more than 90° in the bow. But it works through twice that arc in the stern (180°).

7. *Scull.* This stroke is used in the stern only. It's meant for sneaking, and just possibly it is the most "Indian" of all aboriginal strokes. It's useless except for sneaking, but it is an element of good canoeing.

If you're a total novice, please understand that the bow is the front end of the canoe and the stern (the back end) must follow it. The gunwales are the top edges of the sides. Gunwale is pronounced GUNnel in salty vernacular. Actually, the aboriginals don't call canoe parts much of anything, so far as I have been able to determine.

Now come the detailed descriptions of each stroke.

1. *Forward Stroke.* You hold the paddle natu-rally, fingers of your upper hand over the knob, fingers of your lower hand on the paddle shaft a convenient couple of inches or so above the blade. Keep your lower arm straight but not stiff. The thumb of your lower hand should be on the *outside* of the paddle shaft. This thumb position is for your protection. I have seen a paddler's thumbnail knocked off. (But it's your thumb, and I do not insist on this thumb position except while you're learning.) Then, holding the paddle in a way that feels natural, you kneel, your knees comfortably apart, and lean back against a seat or thwart. Keep your back reasonably straight.

Now, dip the paddle conveniently ahead, keeping

This sketch gives you a bird's-eye view of how the paddle blade moves through the water (cross-hatching) and over the water (dotted line) when a bow paddler makes a forward stroke on the left side.

FORWARD

BOW
(FRONT)

At least while you're learning to paddle (and perhaps after that), keep the thumb of your lower hand on the outside of the paddle shaft, as shown here. You'll protect your thumb from possibly having its nail knocked off.

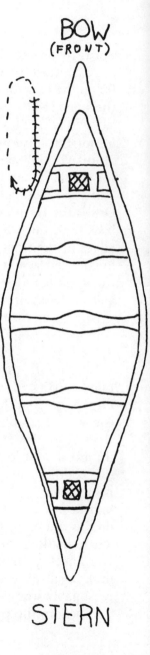

STERN

In doing the forward stroke, you should follow Hap Gilliland's example and draw the paddle back by pushing with your upper arm and pulling with your lower arm.

This paddle's blade has not disappeared. It has been turned parallel to the water (feathered) for the recovery phase of the stroke by turning the inside edge of the paddle toward the stern, which of course turns the outside edge toward the bow.

the width of the blade perpendicular to the centerline of the canoe. Draw the paddle back by pushing with your upper arm and pulling with your lower arm. When you have drawn the paddle conveniently back, turn the inside edge of the blade toward the stern, swish the blade out of the water, and feather it forward through the air, parallel to the water. When the paddle is conveniently forward, turn it perpendicular to the water, and repeat the process. That is it in Forward paddling, done from any part of the canoe.

The practice of turning the inside edge toward the stern before recovering for a new stroke is rather universal for all strokes. So is the straight lower arm and the thumb outside of the shaft. After you have learned the basics, your thumb has the freedom to be abused as you wish.

2. *Backing Stroke* is almost exactly the reverse of Forward. But that lower arm may bend some. You simply reach back with the paddle and push forward against the water. The inside edge of the paddle turns to the stern as you woosh the paddle out of the water to swing it backward through the air to prepare for the next stroke. Backing is very easy and hard to do wrong.

3. *Draw Stroke* is also basically easy and simple. You reach the paddle out from the side of the canoe and paw the paddle toward the canoe in complete strokes. Or you can always do the Draw with the paddle under water, knifing it outward edgewise,

Here's a bird's-eye view of how the paddle blade moves through the water (cross-hatching) and over the water (dotted line) when a bow paddler makes a backing stroke on the left side.

BOW

BACKWARD

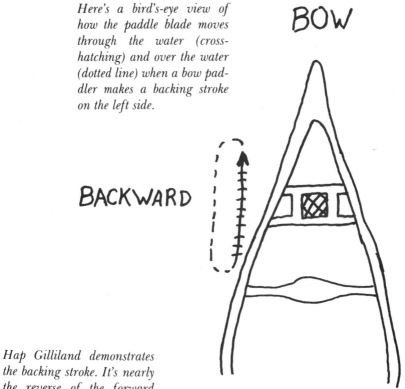

Hap Gilliland demonstrates the backing stroke. It's nearly the reverse of the forward stroke in all respects and is hard to do wrong.

The idea in the draw stroke is to reach out from the side of the canoe, put the paddle into the water, and pull the canoe toward the paddle (as you pull the paddle toward the canoe). The draw can be done in any of three ways: 1) in complete strokes (pulling the paddle blade underwater but returning it through the air), 2) in modified complete strokes (in which you pull the blade underwater but then return it underwater by knifing it outward edgewise), or 3) by wobbling the blade back and forth with constant pressure, a convenient distance from the canoe.

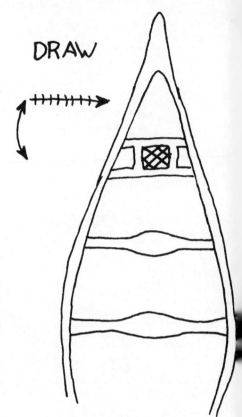

DRAW

Pierre Pulling demonstrates the simplest form of the draw: reaching out from the side of the canoe and pawing the paddle toward the canoe (which moves the canoe toward the paddle).

drawing it back as in the regular Draw. A third Draw method is to reach out and wobble the blade back and forth, in a sort of reverse scull, always keeping the paddle a convenient distance from the canoe and getting most of the pressure from the lower hand. This is the neatest of the three Draw methods but needs study and practice.

4. *Push-over* is extremely simple if you follow instructions. And it's the most powerful stroke because it uses direct leverage. You knife the blade into the water edgewise at right angles to the centerline of the canoe and with the shaft straight up and touching the gunwale. Turn the inside edge of the blade astern, and then pry. The gunwale is your fulcrum. If you are sitting instead of kneeling, you may well use your hip (rather than the gunwale) for the fulcrum. Your wrist is bent out and your fingers are bent in. (For some unknown reason, green paddlers almost always turn the outside edge of the paddle back and fingers out. That's a serious error that lessens power.)

5. *Stern Steering Stroke* is the most important in canoeing. You start as in the Forward Stroke. But then you do a modified Push-over as the blade feathers out. There is no ruddering. The blade normally turns through 90°. The Push-over finish steers the canoe. The blade recovery above water is a convex arc, not concave. You make the recovery as close to the water as is practicable. If in recovery the blade happens to cut through a wave, it is not important. The paddle at that part of the stroke is moving edgewise.

FRONT

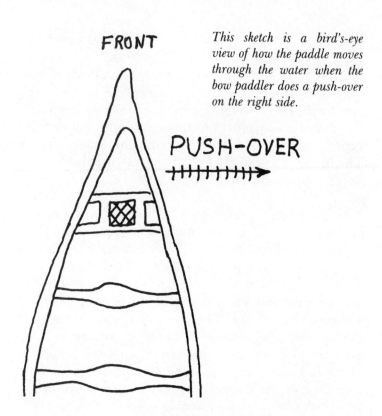

This sketch is a bird's-eye view of how the paddle moves through the water when the bow paddler does a push-over on the right side.

PUSH-OVER

++++++++++++➤

Here's a view of Hap Gilliland doing what the push-over diagram shows. If you are sitting instead of kneeling, you may prefer to use your hip (instead of the gunwale) as the fulcrum for this powerful prying stroke.

When the paddle blade is as far back in the stern steering stroke as you can easily push it, the blade has been turned flat (parallel to the canoe) and the shaft of the paddle is touching the canoe's gunwale, as Pierre Pulling demonstrates.

In this sketch you have a bird's-eye view of the paddle blade's approximate path through the water (cross-hatching) and through the air (dotted line) when the stern paddler uses the stern steering stroke on the left side. Any stroke, of course, can be done on either side.

STERN STEERING

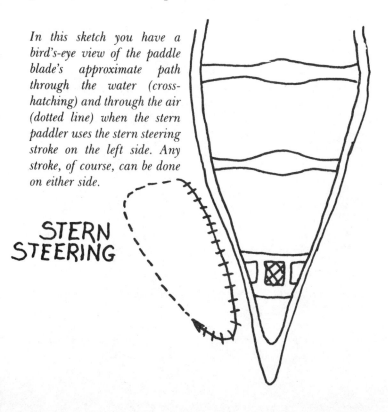

As you pry down with the upper hand, just about like doing the push-over, you begin to swish the blade forward.

In the recovery phase of the stern steering stroke, you start to turn the paddle blade parallel to the water.

Paddle blade moves in a convex arc through the air. At this stage it is almost perfectly parallel to the water. The blade's normal outer edge is forward.

Indian paddlers did not work harder than necessary. Lazy or efficient? You decide. Anyway, if you paddle a 10-hour day, by 4 P.M. you begin to use more back power and less arm power. That's something to logically study. As you paddle, you bend forward and sway back. And unless you are paddling desperately, the stroke is smooth and does not show effort. Any stroke has only the power you put into it, but tension is avoided as much as possible.

6. *The Sweep* is like reaching out with a broom to sweep the chickens off the kitchen porch. The stroke is only 90° in the bow, and a sort of half circle in the stern.

7. *The Scull,* a sort of fishtail propulsion, is very easy to demonstrate but hard to describe. The Scull is usually unimportant but is right clever and quiet. The paddle-motion is always nearly flat. Good canoeists, like good oarsmen, can scull.

There is little or nothing that can be done in propelling a canoe that you cannot do best with these seven strokes. Of course, anyone will invent modifications if there is enough varied experience. Just once I saw a very experienced Ontario guide use a Cross Draw while demonstrating alone in a tricky rapids. He simply changed sides without changing hands. I have done the same, wondering if it was quicker in results than a Push-over on the original side.

The seven strokes I've listed are all those I believe are worth naming. It's ironic that the best canoeists I have seen in action had no names for paddling strokes, so far as I know. They started young.

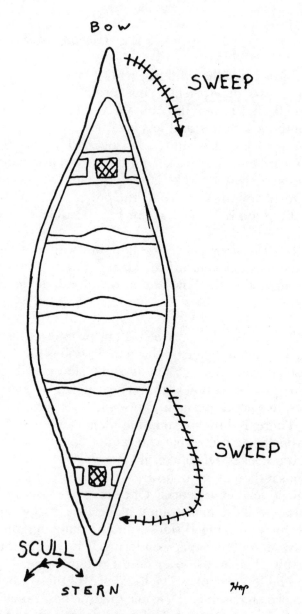

BOW

SWEEP

SWEEP

SCULL

STERN

This sketch shows three stroke variations: 1) the bow sweep, 2) the stern sweep, and 3) the scull, a sort of fishtail stroke.

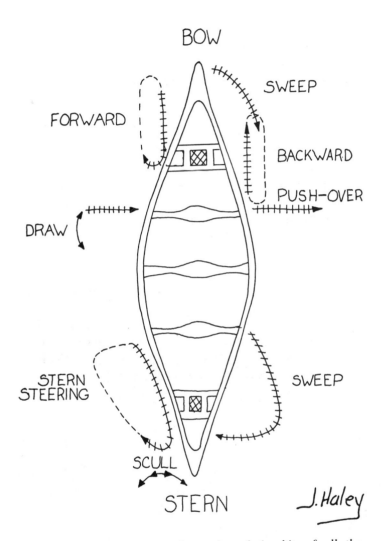

BOW

FORWARD

SWEEP

BACKWARD

PUSH-OVER

DRAW

STERN STEERING

SWEEP

SCULL

STERN

J. Haley

This combination diagram shows the relationship of all the previously demonstrated strokes to the canoe and to each other. In reality, the draw and push-over are sketched a bit too far back so as not to interfere with the sketches of other strokes.

I have trained six-year-olds to be good paddlers and to be very good by age eight. The aboriginals started young and hung tough. The rules were as vague as those for a ranch youngster on a pony at age three.

When I'm working person-to-person with an aspiring paddler, I can usually teach all the theory there is in an hour. Reading will do almost as well if you pay close attention.

A few little kinks in canoe paddling are largely a matter of choice or judgment resulting from practice. For instance, I recommend kneeling because it is safer and conducive to more power. But if the canoe is loaded, sitting is no peril. When you sit in a canoe, cross your feet and tuck them under the seat to take up minimum space. Indian canoes had no seats, so they generally had no sitting problems.

Perhaps you can get accustomed to kneeling on the hard bottom, but I like a kneeling cushion. A life jacket (or personal flotation device, as it's often called these days) shouldn't be used for kneeling. It's the wrong shape, and your kneeling is likely to damage it.

6

Important Canoeing Specialties

Portaging

Among the greatest advantages of a canoe is its portability. Even the vast freighters with 5-ton capacity were built to be carried. And, of course, the cargo was portable.

There's no need here to discuss lugging the really big canoes. The biggest we need to consider may be Grumman's 20-foot jobs, which are semi-freighters or semi-war canoes. And, unless you can find a superman, it will take two canoeists to carry such a canoe. When my wife was running all-girl canoe trips out of Wisconsin's Clearwater Camp, they carried canoes across short portages, four or more girls on each canoe. The canoes were rightside up, and the campers lifted from the thwarts.

Here I will reiterate that I consider canoe lugging a

man's job. I would be the last to say that a woman cannot carry any ordinary canoe. But few women can do it without undue punishment.

I have also briefly discussed yokes. I reemphasize the tumpline. In fact, I'd say that all packs, if the load is 40 pounds or more, rate such a headband. Women can manage packs about as well as men, but few women like tumplines. Maybe they fear developing bull necks.

In any event, the canoe portager must first get the canoe onto his shoulders. Until you become highly skilled, you can start by rolling it up on something and then get under it. Or get someone to help. Good portages—if they're more than a ¼ mile—should have lashed cross-poles or marked trimmed tree limbs on which you can rest the front of the canoe while you take a breather. I have often lugged a canoe a mile without a rest, but I don't recommend it.

In general, you pick up the canoe from the right side, if you are right-handed. You raise it up onto your left thigh so that the yoke is pointing to your left hip. So balanced, you give the canoe a sharp boost with your left knee. Your right hand is holding the left gunwale, and your right arm is almost straight. Your left hand holds the near (right) gunwale, and your left elbow is bent, holding with a biceps pull.

As your left knee boosts the canoe sharply, you let your left hand release the gunwale. And as the canoe rolls over, you crook your left elbow under the gunwale to help with the turning boost. The canoe should come up and over, the yoke dropping around your neck.

This maneuver must be done quickly and smoothly. But an ordinary man, with a little practice, can pick up an 85-pound canoe and walk off with it. Canoe lugging is perhaps the hardest portaging. It can be very difficult or even impossible in the open during a bad wind. Most long portages are in the woods, where the flies don't add to your comfort.

If you use a tumpline on your yoke, your hands grab the tumpline and you extend your elbows under the gunwales to maintain balance. It is a tough routine until you get accustomed to it. You will welcome the end of the portage, but packing will not kill you if you're in good health and you take things gradually.

Let me reiterate the tumpline's helpfulness on portages. And remember that Lieutenant Landman mentioned 90-pound packs. And none heavier. In a pinch, with cargo that was hard to divide, I have carried 140 pounds on a long portage by using a tumpline with no shoulder straps. That much weight was plenty. At the time I was 41 years old. I was 5 feet 9 inches tall and weighed about 150 pounds. Average size. Anyone bigger and stronger can carry more but will also push the canoe deeper into the water.

John McPhee, in his canoe book, discusses the voyageurs of the fur trade. He agrees with the prevalence of 90-pound packs and allows the men were smallish then. McPhee also says that they doubled and trebled on packs. This claim I am inclined to doubt unless the voyageurs were stunting. I knew of a very powerful Indian who carried 300 pounds (weighed and not guessed) over a portage. I saw (in France) a Chinese laborer carry a crate of plug tobacco, net 350 pounds (maybe 375 including the crate). It was tilted onto his back out of a boxcar, and he did not lug it far. If a good voyageur lugged two bales of 90 pounds each, he was carrying enough. My reading, such as it has been, suggests that the voyageurs were generally young, averaged 150 pounds, and were very stocky and muscular. They were tough.

The great advantage of using a tumpline and shoulder straps in combination is the ability you have to slightly alter weight pressures. You may tighten up on the shoulder straps a trifle to ease your head and neck. Or you can just duck your head and it will take more weight. I can manage a 25 percent bigger load with the tumpline plus shoulder straps than I can with shoulder straps alone.

Packing is very hard physical work, but packing is also largely a state of mind. You can do it if you decide you can. Before I end this packing description, I must cite one of Lloyd Melville's experiences back in 1929.

Lloyd was guiding a party in the Algoma District of Ontario when he met some big boys on a portage. They were led—really led—by a tall young man who was playing a harmonica and carrying nothing else. He explained that the boys worked better to some lively music. This chap with the harmonica had solved his own portaging problem admirably.

Poling

You will recall that Lieutenant Landman's voyageurs each had a 10-foot pole "of good ash," with two steel tips. It is possible to pole in a sort of double-paddle style. But the best polers I have known on New Brunswick's Tobique River used only a single steel socket. Their poles were spruce, and usually about 12 feet. I favor their views. Ash can produce a slimmer pole, but thicker spruce is fine for my big hands.

Poling—upstream of course—is very hard work. You usually go down with just the paddle, though downstream pole-snubbing has advantages. You can stop progress with a pole and make a right-angle turn.

Poling, though very tiring, is graceful and efficient. In fact, a really high-class poler is poetry in motion. With little or no instruction, you can learn to pole well enough to get by.

The Tobique polers had describable form: you need a big canoe, 18 feet or longer, and with no keel or with a shoe keel. Most pro polers used 20-foot canoes.

In an otherwise empty craft, you stand so that the bow rides a bit high. If you have a passenger or 200 pounds of freight (which is plenty), you stand just in front of the rear seat, facing toward the poling side (left in my case) and feet spread a bit. You lift the pole with your left hand (let's assume 2 feet of water) and drop the pole's bottom end conveniently forward. Then you grasp the pole conveniently high with your right hand, push back and crouch, and finish with a hard jab.

For the next stroke, the left hand lifts without appreciably changing its pole grasp. The right hand helps guide the pole forward, and the stroke is repeated. I emphasize that in ordinary water this overhand stroke leaves my left hand's position on the pole almost stable. (Of course, you reverse hand positions if you pole on the right side.)

Come deep water, the pole must be "climbed" to some extent, and sort of flung up for the next stroke. Deep water makes poling harder. If the water's too deep, you obviously cannot pole at all. Nor can you paddle against a deep, swift current. Usually there is shallow water on one side of any big, swift stream, but not always.

In really shallow upstream navigation, the steersman can pole with his paddle by turning it edgewise. Then the bow paddler does most of the steering. For this work, I like a paddle slightly longer than usual and made of hardwood. I have seen bateaux paddles with a three-pronged steel tip for this combination work. I'm sad to say I do not have such a paddle. It would be very useful negotiating some swift-but-shallow creeks where we jump-shoot mallards. Probably one small spike on a paddle would do.

For poling in weedy swamps, the lower end of your pole should have a duck-bill tip. You stand and pole, getting along in 6 inches of water if the load is light. I have heard that a good poler can travel a dusty road if someone goes ahead with a sprinkling can, but I am not that good.

Just as U.S. voyageurs have neglected tumplines,

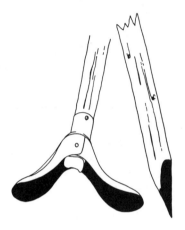

The lower end of a canoe pole can vary considerably according to circumstances. The duck-bill (left) is used where the waterway's bottom is soft. If you must cut a pole in an emergency, its lower end will look something like the one at the right. A pole that's rigged specifically for a rocky bottom may have a metal tip (not shown).

they also have neglected poles. I believe that poles deserve more attention.

Common sense further suggests that you can get on fairly well without a metal pole tip. In an emergency, you go ashore, cut a pole, and use it. Such a rig won't be as effective as a pole that's been peeled, dried, sandpapered, and oiled, as your real pole should be. A canoe pole is great not only for poling but also for use as a tent pole.

Transporting

I have a two-canoe trailer made essentially of welded black-iron pipe. The canoes ride one above the other, suspended on slings of heavy belting. On this rig, my canoes ride rightside up, taking in water if it rains. You can't have everything. They do ride better than when hung upside down. For short rides on smooth roads, I just let the canoes hang in their slings. If the distance is long or the roads rough, I tie them to prevent their working ahead. Any load tends to work ahead.

By towing this trailer and placing my third canoe on top of the truck, I can move my whole flotilla easily. With a helper, I can load or unload the works in 5 minutes.

Though we see all manner of boat trailers, I know of no commercial canoe trailer. Idaho State University's Outdoors Office has a bigger trailer than mine. Any master welder can make one. Mine has old Ford car springs, but I do not have exact specifications. My trailer was designed, as it was built, by a welding student. But a very competent mechanical-engineering professor, the late Abe Lillibridge, furnished the brains. I have yet to induce a canoe manufacturer to develop good trailers, but I still hope I can.

What about carrying a canoe on a car? I'm a bit skeptical about the common clamp-on rooftop carriers. I know of two instances in which a canoe flew off the top of a car. The flight did the canoe no good and was most hazardous to drivers of following cars. I didn't see these incidents happen, but I saw the sad canoes later.

I have a 4 x 4-inch block fitted to the roof of my pickup's cab with 2 ringbolts on each end. The canoe is held in place with 2-inch webbing straps and friction buckles. My pickup's rear bracket is built of welded black-iron pipe and fitted with a rubber-covered roller. Front and rear straps are identical. For a passenger car, I recommend two fitted 4 x 4-inch blocks.

This rig holds a canoe. For many years while I was a federal refuge biologist, a canoe was as essential as binoculars. I have trucked one as far as 10,000 miles a year. As I write, a canoe is on my pickup. I may jump ducks tomorrow. My 15-foot Grumman will ride in the truck bed. At age 87 and after hernia surgery, I do not put a canoe up on a truck alone unless there is no help available. You are not that old! But help always lightens the task of loading canoes for the road.

Towing

I have mixed feelings about motorboats. They are often misused, but still they have their legitimate uses. One valid use is to tow a canoe or as many as half a dozen. The motor doesn't get tired.

A canoe, or a couple of canoes one behind the other, can be easily and safely towed by bridles. If you are dragging two, the lead canoe rates a bridle on each end. The pull must come at or below the waterline in order to avoid capsizing the canoes.

For towing six canoes, we rigged them in three

The author's pickup truck is about ready to roll with an aluminum canoe on its roof rack. The truck also tows a trailer that has a bark canoe (top) and a fiberglass canoe (bottom). Note that canoe on roof rack is upside down but that those on trailer are slung on heavy belting and ride rightside up.

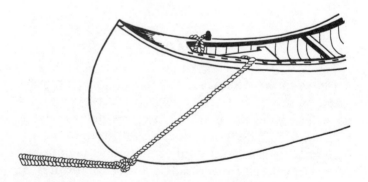

The trick in towing a canoe is to make sure the pull is exerted at the waterline or below it. A bridle such as the one shown here does the job nicely.

"teams" resembling catamarans. The front team had a 2 x 6-inch plank lashed across the stern seats, and an upright bracket was bolted onto it for mounting the motor. Dry poles were lashed across the thwarts of all three "teams," and poles were lashed at angles so that each team would be rigid.

It takes some experimenting to get the canoes the right distances apart. If they're too close together from side to side or one pair follows another at too short a distance, full speed may cause the canoes to ship water. We towed these rigs great distances, including from Fort Albany to Moose Factory on James Bay in salt water.

It takes about an hour to get such a contraption assembled—longer if you must hunt and cut poles. But a 3½ horsepower outboard made maybe 5 miles an hour and kept at it. Sometimes we helped by paddling, and sometimes each canoe needed a bailer.

Canoeing Etiquette

Possibly Quebec woodsmen, both Indian and white, are the most courteous people in the world. Anyway, there is a Canoe Code, or there used to be. If it has deteriorated, it should be brought back.

One of the simple courtesies—when canoe parties pass—is to drift past each other with paddles across the gunwales. If there is no other reason for communication, one says, "Quay, quay." I do not know exactly what "quay" means, nor is it important. It is proper.

In addition to the salutation, it is a good idea for leaders to tell each other where they are going and for how long. People need each other in wilderness areas. If parties are not too large, camping together may be pleasant. There are things to swap and tales to tell.

On one trip in Maine, I was with an all-girl party. The weather was wet. We camped near another all-girl party, and they lacked an axeman. The leader of this other party had been struggling to cook. There was a grove of dry spruces handy.

As soon as we got reasonably well established, I sent one of my campers over with an armload of dry split spruce. This other leader—I forget both her name and camp—actually shed tears of gratitude. I cut all the dry spruce they needed. It was no problem. Routine canoe-trip courtesy.

Upstream Paddling

If a current is buckable at all with a paddle, the stream usually has navigable water on one side or the other. Also, the slower water usually is on the inside of the curves. You stay on that inside. It may have eddies that actually push the canoe upstream. So you should cut points closely.

In currents that cannot be negotiated by either paddle or pole, you may be able to "line" or "track" upstream. A "V" line or "Y" line may be attached to the bow and stern of a canoe. If such a line is rigged right, your pull on the stern keeps the bow from coming ashore. In some instances, having a poler aboard is a help. Lewis and Clark "lined" their boats for hundreds of miles.

And thinking back to Lieutenant Landman, I imagine that his 10-man crew was maybe half poling and half dragging with "hambro" lines. I'd guess four men aboard with the poles and six on the line. The lieutenant probably walked the shore in dignity when he chose, or just sat and rode.

Judgment and experience pay off in current bucking. Up to a point, you can seemingly defy physical laws. The canoe is slippery, and you can ease it along upstream when you know how.

Loading

Loading rules are simple. The first rule is to avoid overloading. What is correct for certain weather conditions can be dangerous or fatal if the weather changes. You take advantage of good conditions such as those in early morning. Or if the weather turns favorable after a bad spell, you might decide to paddle all night.

If you must buck a wind, the bow should be somewhat heavy. The reverse is true if you have a tail wind. When you travel downstream in rather fast water, the bow should always be a bit light. Going downstream against wind is very tricky navigation. The wind will swing the canoe. At a time like that, you must either be very careful or not go at all.

One of the most tragi-comic scenes is to watch a

green paddler fighting a breeze while sitting on the rear seat. He seems to believe that since the seat is there, he must use it. Of course, he doesn't get anywhere and doesn't know why.

Shelters for Canoeists

I am often asked about how to protect canoeists from the weather.

Probably those tough voyageurs who worked for Lieutenant Landman or were written about by John McPhee used tents seldom or never. I will risk a substantial wager, though, that the lieutenant had a private tent.

Probably a tarp was stretched over the upturned canoe and the crew got under it if the weather was wet. A couple of people can sleep (head to head) under an 18-foot canoe and stay reasonably dry. And a stretched tarp will still make-do.

I have been with organized camps that ran trips with no tents. The kids rigged poncho shelters and what-not if they bothered at all. I always had my own smallish tent, maybe 7 x 7 feet, to keep food dry. Occasionally, come the sudden midnight shower, I have been awakened by the whole party trying to get into my tent. Campers, especially girls, like to sleep under the "gorgeous" stars. So do I if the stars stay out. When they vanish and the sky drips, it's a different ballgame. So I always vote for tents—as light as practicable—for use all over the East and North.

Much of the West stays dry enough all summer. But if you get into high country, any sort of weather may develop. Earlier I mentioned my four summers as a ranger on Yellowstone Park's Shoshone Lake. I'd see as many as 30 canoes on it at one time. Some of the canoeists had tents, some didn't. Almost 8,000 feet up, showers and even steady two-day rains were common. And usually we got appreciable snow in late June and always by August 25. Mosquitoes were also serious, though they usually were frozen out by 9 P.M. and it didn't warm up until 8 A.M. or later. They might freeze out for days, but they lasted into September when the weather was mild. Tents are most logical under such conditions. I have taken canoe trips without a tent, for the simple reason that I had no tent. But I don't recommend tentless canoe trips.

7

Canoeing for the Sportsman and Woodsman

Though the hunter or fisherman might, by careful reading, glean most of the information he needs from other parts of this book, he deserves a chapter on special points about his canoeing. Yet this chapter might be helpful to anyone who takes canoe trips.

The sportsman paddles his canoe, poles it, tows it, and observes safety precautions just as any other canoeist does. Carrying valuable guns makes him especially careful about avoiding a spill. Besides, we jump-shoot mallards into January when the water is extremely cold and we're not at all eager for a dunking.

The sportsman selects his canoe with his special needs in mind. He will usually demand a rugged craft.

The Hunter's Canoe

My Canadian experience showed me that, over thousands of square miles, practically no hunting boats except canoes were in use. Furthermore, the hunters were as skilled as hunters anywhere.

I firmly insist that all sportsmen's needs for a hand-propelled or even a light-motor-propelled boat may be met by some type of canoe. However, it takes the exception to prove the rule, and those of us who are trained in the natural sciences must admit that exceptions exist. The exception in hunting boats might be the highly specialized sinkbox of the water-fowl hunter in coastal marshes that have little vegetation above the water.

Where there is any appreciable cover, a canoe is just as easy to conceal as any other boat and is better in all other respects, so far as my experience indicates. I spent five years in the Mississippi River bottoms of Minnesota and Wisconsin and have made close observations in Canada. I carefully compared canoes with all manner of other duck boats.

For the ordinary hunter, I recommend a medium-size, sturdy canoe. My old Prospector model, made by the Canadian Canoe Company of Peterboro, Ontario, could not be improved on for a party of two. It is 16 feet long, has a 36-inch beam, and is 14 inches deep. This canoe has 4 inches of freeboard with a load of 850 pounds. The canoe itself weighs 85 pounds clean and dry—5 pounds more with an attached yoke and one paddle.

Another very satisfactory canoe that I used on the Upper Mississippi Wildlife Refuge was a slightly shallower but longer craft, made by the E.M. White Canoe Company of Old Town, Maine. White canoes are no longer made. It was a Guide's Special, 18½ feet long, about the same weight as the Prospector.

Both of these canoes were made of canvas-covered cedar. The canvas was painted about the color of dead marsh vegetation. Mammals—excepting man and some apes—may all be color blind, but waterfowl are not handicapped by any impairments of vision. Some duck hunters do careful camouflage paint jobs on their canoes. This is a matter of individual preference, which needs no comment here except to note that the paint should not shine.

If an aluminum canoe is used (I use little else now), it should be painted or partly painted. A somewhat weathered aluminum canoe with dull-green markings of standard camouflage type is very inconspicuous.

You rarely worry about the noise of an aluminum craft while duck hunting. But if you are sneaking up a creek to enter the territory of a smart whitetail buck, the canvas-covered canoe has advantages. Such use is the only sporting activity I can envision in which I believe the aluminum craft is at a serious disadvantage compared to one of cedar and canvas.

Under certain circumstances, with two or more hunters working together, a 20-foot Guide's model is not out of place. In general, however, only one hunter should shoot from a canoe or any other small boat while it is in motion. If the canoe is hidden in the tules, two hunters may shoot while sitting back to back.

In some places, duck boats are very popular. I certainly do not want to injure duck-boat sales, but I have never seen anything done with a duck boat that I could not do more easily with a canoe. Furthermore, the canoe is more versatile for other purposes. My old Canadian has been used for fishing and cruising from its native Ontario through Michigan, Wisconsin, Minnesota, Montana, Nevada, California, Oregon, Idaho, and Wyoming. It has also been used to help in hunting ducks, geese, pheasant, deer, and various "varmints."

The pheasant shooting was largely done along the Milk River in Montana while I was stationed on what is now the Charles Russell Game Range. The Milk is a slow, meandering little stream, flanked by almost impenetrable brush. Smart cock pheasants would hop from one bank to the other, quite safe from brush-foundered hunters. But when we hunted as a party of four, one on each bank and two in the canoe, those cocks were hopping right in front of the bow gunner. He got all of the shooting, of course, so we had to take turns. The birds generally fell in the water, where we easily retrieved them.

Even on some pretty big water, the canoe has real advantages as a hunting craft. My experience on the

Mississippi above Winona, Minnesota, where I was biologist for the Upper Mississippi Refuge, is a good example. The river comes down through three great "pools"—the Winona, the Whitman, and the Alma— that are formed by the dams of the Nine Foot Channel, built in the 1930s. Ducks congregate on these waters, sometimes on one, sometimes on another, sometimes on all three. You never know where they are until you look. Frequently they're here today and gone tomorrow.

This state of affairs made life difficult for one of my associates, whom I will call Mr. Smith. He liked duck hunting, and he had a boat all right. It was a good solid craft to shoot from, since it was modeled more or less on the lines of a baby flattop. It was so cumbersome that it took four strong men and a boy to hoist it onto a truck or unload it into the water. Once it reached an anchorage, that was it for the season. Shifting it was an advanced maritime operation much too complicated to be done more than once a year.

You couldn't move it overland from channel to channel. You couldn't pole it through a sticky marsh. You couldn't even row it faster than a mile an hour unless you were really straining. Smith ran it with a sizable outboard motor, which limited his operations to the deeper sloughs. He made the mistake of putting this barge down in the Winona Pool one year when the ducks chose to avoid that water. There he had to hunt right through the season, though often there wasn't a quacker within a country mile.

Meanwhile, my canoe allowed me to get around in these pools at my pleasure. I could cross all three of them in one day quite easily. I could snatch my 85-pound Guide's model from channel to channel. I could pole or drag her across shallows or muddy marshes, and I could paddle her across open water. Of equal importance, I could start all even with Mr. Smith at the close of the shooting day and then pole or paddle my canoe to the parking place much quicker than he could attach his eggbeater and come in under power. I leave it to you to guess who had the better shooting that year.

At this point I should note that it is not legal to shoot from a boat propelled by any means except manual power. This has long been a federal law on migratory-bird shooting, and I believe that all the states and all the Canadian provinces have similar statutes. In most instances, law-enforcement officers consider that any boat or canoe with a motor attached is motor-propelled. So you cannot shoot from an outboard-equipped craft unless you detach the motor from the stern and bring it inboard. At one time the Minnesota authorities would not even permit shooting from a boat if an outboard engine was lying flat in its bottom. But this law was changed, and I never heard of any other so strict.

It is easy to mount an outboard motor on any canoe that's big enough for hunting, but it is rare for the canoe hunter to really need a motor. Putt-putting the canoe is just transportation. The outboard is most valuable if you use it only to go to the shooting area before shooting hours and to return after the day ends. A good canoe hunter should get his limit of ducks in less time than that if the ducks are moving.

In Idaho, since 1948, some of our deadliest duck shooting has been done from a moving canoe. The bow gunner is eligible to shoot as soon as anything is within range. When or if he paddles, he should have a strong cord some 4 feet long with one end tied around the middle of the paddle and the other end fastened through the gunwale or around a thwart on the paddling side. Then he can safely drop his paddle and grab his gun if a duck jumps.

It is obviously much faster if the bow gunner is not paddling and is already holding his gun. I have occasionally jump-shot alone in a canoe, by dropping the paddle and grabbing a gun. The unpaddled canoe swings, so this is a difficult type of hunting.

An old Canadian hunters' trick is to put a screen of balsam boughs in the bow of the canoe and drift downwind or down current. A good paddler can steer the canoe and even make some deadwater progress by sculling, never taking the paddle out of the water and making only the most limited hand motions. Sculling is something that anyone can learn.

The hunter's canoe should be equipped with a built-in carrying yoke. The equipment should include not only paddles but also an ordinary setting pole and a duck-bill pole. A good bow ring, with a canoe-length $\frac{3}{8}$-inch rope attached, is desirable on any canoe and is essential for hunting. You often need it to tie up.

For waterfowling, a canoe dog is very useful if you're jumping birds on creeks or small rivers that have brushy shores. Any breed of dog can be taught to sit quietly. It pleases the dog to pick ducks from the water over the canoe's edge. And he will watch for drifting birds to start down. Bigger dogs must be more carefully trained. A dog that dances or wriggles will put the gunner off. Well-trained dogs love to canoe ride. Of course the smaller retrievers are less weight to lug. And swimming is not important. The canoe does that. Birds that land on shore are the problem. A dog generally enables us to get every bird that falls.

The Fisherman's Canoe

Nearly any canoe suitable for hunting is just as suitable for fishing, but some fishermen insist on an outboard motor while the hunter rarely needs one. Many anglers would do better if they paddled more and motored less. Pollution rates attention, too.

Canoes are frequently used to work out from big motorboats. My old Canadian canoe has been in on the taking of many a bass on the Nevada side of Lake Mead. We lugged the canoe across as a deck load, and then we used it to fish the less-fished areas well away from the landing near Boulder City. We have done the same on Hudson Bay and Lake Superior. On Hudson Bay, two freight canoes were carried lashed to the stays of a 45-foot auxiliary schooner. The canoes were used as lighters and tenders, as well as for hunting and fishing.

A word may be in order here on folding canoes and rubber rafts and boats. Folding canoes, or collapsible boats of any sort, can be lugged into a remote region on a pack animal or even on a human back. Experienced packers have put everything from kitchen stoves to pianos on pack mules, but I have yet to see an animal pack a real canoe. It might be done, but I started horse-packing 30 years too late to try it.

Though the folding and pneumatic boats have their places, I do not want to use them any more than I have to. But anything that will float may come in handy for fishing.

Years ago in eastern Canada, it was a common practice to make a dugout canoe—also called a log canoe or pirogue—on a remote lake and leave it there when the fishing trip was over. I have seen fine pirogues made from aspen, arborvitae, and Western red cedar. In the South, I know that such craft have been made from tulip poplar, bald cypress, and red gum. Tropical natives make dugouts from many types of hardwood. An axe, an auger, and an adze are the only tools required to make a pirogue. I have seen good ones made with only an axe and a crooked knife. Aboriginals made them by burning and scraping. As for making one myself, all I have done is talk.

For a lone fisherman or a pair of anglers, my Prospector has done as well for fishing as for hunting. Practically all the suggestions for hunting from a canoe apply equally to fishing from one. I believe that inland fish can generally be caught more easily and played more safely from a canoe than from any other floating device. Canoes are not for deep-sea trolling or for fishing the largest lakes, unless they work out from a bigger vessel. But for general sportfishing, no hardship would be experienced if no small boats other than canoes existed—provided, of course, that the users know how to paddle.

Other Practical Specialties

Prospectors, surveyors, game wardens, fire patrol-men, field biologists, trappers, and what-have-you all find the canoe the most useful small boat under most conditions, if it's used with skill.

Army assault boats are essentially canoes, and my heart bleeds to see the way soldiers paddle them. The use of canoes in mobile warfare in wet countries has been badly neglected, and canoes have been equally neglected in certain types of rescue work, especially for downed flyers. Our armed services may not own a real canoe, yet a long chapter if not a small book could well be devoted to the miltiary possibilities of canoes. Like pigeons and dogs, they would always be useful, but so far no one in authority has given them much thought.

8

Canoe Care

Aluminum canoes need little care. They can survive pretty well even without a roof in the winter. The manufacturers wisely suggest, though, that you apply good paint to an aluminum canoe if you intend to use it in salt water.

If an aluminum canoe develops slight seeps along its keel rivets, a smear of waterproof glue inside is a simple cure. There are various epoxy boat glues. Even simpler is Duco cement. And if an actual hole is made in an aluminum canoe, any strong cloth, glued on with Duco, should get it home.

A welder can mend a small crack permanently, or weld on a piece of aluminum—preferably on the inside. Run-of-the-mill welders may not be able to manage aluminum repairs. Here at Idaho State University is an aviation mechanics school in the

Vocational-Technical branch. I haven't needed their help on leaks, but they have corrected manufacturers' mistakes on both aluminum and fiberglass canoes.

An occasional dent may be unavoidable in fast-water travel. Aluminum dents can generally be improved by a rubber mallet.

Fiberglass is less foolproof than aluminum but will stand plenty of weather. My old fiberglass Herter has never been under a roof during its 15 or more years of life. And patching a hole or crack is simple. On a trip I can use a piece of pants leg or shirttail attached by Duco cement or by one of the epoxy glues. Back home I can get a piece of fiberglass cloth and some compatible fiberglass liquid from a good hardware store. Instructions are on the labels. I haven't needed much fiberglass repairing, but it's not hard to learn.

As for canvas canoes, one possibility is that you may find an old one hanging in a garage or in a shed of some organized camp. When my wife and I worked for camps, I managed as many as 30 at one time. Caring for them was an appreciable chore, but I made many a workable craft out of many a sorry wreck.

Canvas patching is simple. The paint should be roughened around the hole with a knife. Then you glue on a patch of relatively light but strong cloth (heavy canvas would make a lump). A simple patch, with a later swipe of spar varnish, may last as long as the rest of the skin.

If there is a slit in the canvas, and this is not unusual, a patch both inside and outside the slit is advisable. Stitching the slit over the inside patch is a good idea if the glue doesn't dry too fast. Then the outside patch really holds.

A common error in the repair of canvas canoes is to use too much paint. Filled canvas deserves some color and smoothing, but I doubt whether any canvas canoe has its life increased by one hour because of painting. If paint is worn on the bottom, spar varnish with a little color may well be applied. And I recommend a touch of spar varnish whenever there is a sign of weather wear or scraping. But paint is heavy stuff, and paint-loaded canvas cracks easily.

On a duck-hunting trip, my old Prospector model blew off the car as I unstrapped it. The mishap cracked three ribs and splintered some planking. But still the canoe didn't leak. Come the end of the season, I took it apart, counted back and noted the appropriate numbers of the ribs, and ordered from the Canadian Canoe Company three new ribs and a square foot of planking. I fitted the ribs, fastened the planking with small copper tacks, and put the contraption together again good as new. It's something practically anyone could do with hand tools. Of course, you put anything together just the reverse of the way you took it apart. But you go slow the first time and take careful note of how you take it apart.

Eventually a canvas skin may become patch-upon-patch. Or if you pick up a badly maintained canoe, it can be paint-loaded. If a paint-loaded canoe has an intact skin, you can loosen the paint with a blow torch and peel the paint. But use a big knife in a shaving motion—not a paint scraper or putty knife. Paint scrapers and putty knives wrinkle the canvas ahead of the knife. The shaving motion works better. I have taken 20 pounds of alligator-cracked paint off of a canoe. Then I refilled and painted it, and the result was very satisfactory. Not as slick as a factory repair, but at a quarter the cost if I don't count my own time.

If you find a canoe that has a fairly intact hull but a hopeless skin, you simply take the canvas off and put on a new covering.

Taking the canvas off requires no tools other than a couple of screwdrivers—perhaps a big one for screws in the gunwales and keel.

New canvas for the ordinary canoe should be No. 8. A big freight canoe or war canoe might better use No. 6. Designations for canvas are something like those used for the sizes of shot: the smaller the number, the heavier the canvas (or the shot).

Any canvas or awning shop has or can readily get the proper canvas. The piece should be maybe 6 inches longer than the canoe, and wide enough to go down around the middle from gunwale to gunwale.

For the recanvassing, your most essential (but very simple) equipment is a pair of wooden clamps. Mine, used for perhaps 25 years, are made from four boards each 2 x 6 x 27 inches. They become clamps by the use of three bolts to hold each pair together. The bolts are ½ inch in diameter and have big washers on each end to prevent the boltheads and nuts from cutting into the timber. A rope hole is bored at the top end of each clamp.

The procedure is to fold the canvas once down the center the long way, pinch both ends of the canvas in the clamps, and then hang the canvas about like a hammock. You'll need to fasten the clamp ropes to overhead timbers or to tree limbs—something very solid.

Sketch shows some of the key ingredients in a do-it-yourself job of replacing the skin on a cedar-and-canvas canoe. A clamp (made of two boards) at each end of the new canvas allows you to get the project moving in the right direction.

Now the bare hull of the canoe must be forced into the canvas "hammock" as tight as is practicable. If it shoves in easily, take it out, adjust one clamp to shorten the hammock a bit, and try again.

Once the hull is forced into the hammock as firmly as you can get it, place some weight in the canoe to push the hull down and thereby help shape the canvas to the hull. A warm, dry atmosphere is best. Dampness shrinks cotton, and canvas is cotton.

As soon as the canoe is properly situated in the canvas, you start tacking the canvas to the gunwales. You use the same type of brass or copper tacks that you removed. In fact, you may have saved some of the ones you removed. It is important to start tacking in the middle of the canoe and gradually work in both directions on both sides. Follow the previous spacing of tacks. It helps to have a tacker on each side. In fact, two people can work together rather well on many phases of this job.

When the tacking has reached close to the ends, the canoe must be removed from the clamps. Then, one worker pulls the canvas across the stern while the other worker tacks the canvas there. Next, the canvas is trimmed with a sharp jackknife, filler is smeared on the stern, and the other side of the canvas is pulled tight and tacked. It also is trimmed. Follow the same procedure at the bow end.

You are now ready for the filler.

Manufacturers of canvas canoes use "secret" filler material, and sometimes you can buy it. But I doubt whether anything is better than a mixture of whiting and spar varnish. Whiting is the chalky powder that's used in the making of ordinary putty for holding window glass.

The filler mix should be the consistency of rather thick paint and can be smeared on with a fairly big brush. The filler should really fill the canvas. It will dry hard as bone overnight. Then the outside gunwales and metal stem bands should be screwed on. A light sanding of the filled canvas with No. 0 sandpaper will result in a smoother base for the paint.

Deck paint, or porch-floor paint, is OK for a canvas

canoe. Linseed-oil paint (lead-and-oil) was once standard and is all right if sweetened with perhaps a quarter spar varnish. Actual canoe enamel is available. It's fine but fairly expensive. Linseed-oil paint on unfilled canvas rots the fabric. Linseed-oil paint is not as common as it was, and I don't mourn its decline. Your paint dealer will advise you cheerfully. One painting is enough, for keeps. A swipe of spar varnish on the bottom should compensate for any wear. But if you are careful there should not be much wear. A canvas canoe, even though it's used a lot, will last many years if it's treated kindly. Nevertheless, re-covering may be required in 10 or 12 years.

If the canoe has a keel (unfortunately) it is screwed on from the inside. You put it back just as you took it off. But if it was a standard deep keel, I suggest that you try to get a shallow shoe keel from the manufacturer.

There are old canvas canoes kicking around here and there. You may manage to turn one of them into a good one with a little rebuilding. Canvas canoes approach the Indian's birch-bark jobs in construction and are quiet. They demand a fair amount of care but are worth it.

9

Sidelights of
Canoeing History

Some amazing peculiarities have occurred in U.S. canoeing. I was there to see a considerable part of it, so I include what I know.

There is no reason to dwell further on early U.S. canoeing. Explorers picked it up from the Indians. It is likely that most paddling was done well in those days.

Just when paddling began to deteriorate is a moot question, but deteriorate it did. I was raised in the Hudson Highlands of New York State. I went to high school in Poughkeepsie. From an early age, I saw canoeing on the Hudson River and on various streams and lakes. My observations began about 1900, but I did not know enough then to be critical. I used a canoe a little when I was a beginning student at the New York State College of Forestry (now State University of New York College of Environmental Science and Forestry) at Syracuse. I was an undergraduate from 1911 to 1915. And though I was too light for a varsity oarsman, I learned to row in a shell under a great coach, James A. Ten Eyck. However, the paddling I did in those days was sketchy, uncoached, and inefficient.

My work in Quebec was from May 1 into September, 1914. I learned professional Canadian woods paddling. It was vastly different from the grossly poor canoeing I had seen.

When I got out of the woods in 1914, I was basically interested in canoeing as a method of transportation. I gave the subject considerable thought and even coached a little during my senior year in college.

After graduation in 1915, I worked in northern New England and immediately had some association with organized camps. They used canoes extensively, and the paddling was horrible.

Come 1916, I was working as a forester for the Lake Tarleton Club out of Pike, New Hampshire. The club, owning some 8,000 acres on three lakes, leased sites to three organized camps—all for girls. I was a sort of liaison officer between the club administration and the camp directors. I coached canoeing casually, especially at Camp Serrana. In December 1916, I married Gertrude Bassett, niece of Dr. Emma G. Sebring, who was the organizer of this camp.

In the summer of 1917, I was drafted to help "make the world safe for democracy." I went into the

Army on October 3, 1917, and was discharged on April 8, 1919, after 16 months overseas service. I came back to the Lake Tarleton Club temporarily. I was to start teaching September 1 at the University of New Brunswick in Down East, Canada.

During the last week of June 1919, the forerunner of the American Camping Association ran a Water Conference at Camp Tahoma (another Tarleton Club Camp), and I was assigned to help with canoeing. That was the start of a disagreement that was to go on in one way or another for over 55 years.

In charge of canoeing at this conference was a lady named Eleanor Deming. She may or may not have been assisted by another middle-aged woman, M. Elizabeth Bates, and by a rather young niece, both of whom were also closely associated with a bizarre steering stroke they called "The Straight Arm 'J'."

In fairness, I must emphasize that some of the Deming general canoeing had merit. But there was serious inaccuracy in the use of too many and badly named strokes. Straight arms and that "J" would cause the late aboriginal masters to roll in their graves.

This Straight Arm "J" stroke was somewhat a combination of an Olympic racing stroke and a good imagination. Miss Deming had written a little volume, *Handbook For Canoeing Counsellors*. She did not write badly, was a good swimmer, and could sell.

I asked, somewhat flabbergasted, where she had learned this stroke. She said it was an Indian method. I allowed that I had worked with Abenikees, Montagnais, and Hurons and that they did not paddle that way. She went on to explain that this Straight Arm

"J" came from Alaskan Indians. I had not been to
Alaska, so I asked her what tribes.

Then things got a bit thick. Miss Deming had been
no nearer Alaska than I had. But I was not yet 28,
and she was graying and probably fortyish. So I
stayed reasonably courteous. But I believed she was
faking, and I think she knew my thoughts. She also
knew that I was an authentic canoeist. She and I
never became buddies, but we maintained the
amenities.

It was 1925 before I learned any details about the
actual birth of that Straight Arm "J." I won't swear to
its total accuracy but am sure beyond a reasonable
doubt.

Miss Deming and Miss Bates were canoeing counselors in a Maine camp, or just possibly in neighbor-
ing camps. Probably Camp Accomac was the place—
an excellent camp that spawned a nuisance.

Apparently Miss Bates made the paddle motions
(largely inventions out of the blue sky), and Miss
Deming wrote them down. At that time, there was a
developing "Women's Sports" view as opposed to
"Sports for Women." It is likely that this method was
supposed to be feministic. I had assumed canoeing
was sexless as well as ageless, but my Quebec-
oriented view was hopeless before Miss Deming's
superb promotional ability.

In the course of time, the absurdity of keeping
both elbows straight became too conspicuous. But, as
late as 1929 in Wisconsin, I saw it used and defended
as a "war-canoe stroke." Why war canoes demanded
specialized paddling was not explained.

Though the motion of keeping both elbows
straight did not endure, most canoeing writers in the

Lower 48 (myself included) from 1919 to the present have used the term "J" for a steering stroke.

Another historic point I should mention in connection with the final (I hope) demise of the infamous "J" is the multiplicity of strokes spawned along about the same time. One bulletin on my desk, dating back several years, describes some 20 separate strokes.

In my chapter describing strokes, I list four basic ones and three important combination strokes. I can name no others as done by aborigines and associated professional Canadian woodsmen. Truly, there are variations possible in twisty rapids. And if a canoeist wanted to waste time, perhaps all sorts of strokes are describable. A writer can possibly describe, for instance, every motion of a football player returning a punt. But the description would be difficult and largely without merit.

Some of these described strokes, such as the "bow-rudder" types, are useless without steerageway (that is, unless the canoe is moving faster than the water). And in any event, their objectives can be more efficiently accomplished by better strokes. "Cross bow" is another unnecessary stroke. It is harder to do than the routine "Push-over" and is only about half as efficient. I will cheerfully compete.

Another extraneous point is the order that instructors often give to aspiring canoeists: "Never touch the shaft of your paddle to the canoe's gunwale!" A professional woods steersman generally levers his paddle shaft against the gunwale during *every* stroke. Why not, unless the Indians were wrong? Which they were not!

In all phases of canoeing, there should be a reason for everything. One canoeing rule, however, seems a bit arbitrary. Though the both-straight-elbows technique is absurd, the lower arm during most paddling is almost straight. The idea is somewhat parallel to keeping one elbow straight when swinging a golf club. Maybe the method is just more efficient. It is, even if the analysis is rather obscure. Yet no one seems to have analyzed the reason for the edict about no prying on the gunwale. Prying, which obeys the law of the lever, is efficient.

For well over half a century, U.S. canoeing was burdened by a stubborn insistence on fake paddling. Its inventors were informed that it was a fake by the end of that Tahoma Conference in late June of 1919.

Though I'm no sports professional, I have been accused of being a professional canoeist. Furthermore, I am something of a sports fan. I have observed football since the fall of 1906 and have played some. I had seven seasons of high-school and university track competition and have coached running. I rowed a little in a varsity shell. Through the years, I have sat in extensively on hockey, lacrosse, amateur boxing, amateur wrestling, and basketball. Besides, my lifetime has included a fair share of riding, shooting, and flycasting—the shooting and flycasting assisted by canoeing.

I mention this background as an indication of the extent to which I have known various athletic coaches. With the exception of canoeing instructors, the coaches knew their subjects. The canoeists could not paddle. They could swim, however, and they approached canoeing—apparently—from the viewpoint of falling out. All the while they claimed canoeing had an Indian heritage. Yet they refused to consider Indian paddling methods.

Many of the people and organizations who were sold on the Deming "J" and all the absurdities that went with it did not know any better. But Miss Deming and her immediate lieutenants did know better. I told them. And they knew that I knew Indian paddling methods.

I'm happy to report a considerable change for the better in some of the canoeing methods advocated by major national organizations. There will possibly always be a little variation in canoeing strokes. There was a little (very little) among the aboriginals themselves. Despite terrific variations in their canoes and paddles, the aboriginals all used pretty much the same strokes.

These details are on paper for the first time. I never before considered the subject in such written detail. No one elese has bothered. The opposition school talked some and wrote some. I was definitely not their favorite person, but they never accused me of being a poor canoeist. Largely, they emphasized that I "did not understand" their views. And in that respect they were very right; I did not.

So, at long last, the aborigines seem to have just about won. Since I invented nothing, I could win nothing. Back in the 1920s, aboriginal steering, in New England camps, was sometimes called "the Pulling stroke." That was a misnomer, because I copied it 100 percent from the methods of the aborigines.

Definitely, the aborigines and the Venetian gondoliers knew how to paddle. At long last, canoeists in general are beginning to get the message.

10

Canoeing Standards for Organized Camps

My main quarrel with the canoeing standards advocated by major organizations in this country during the past several decades has been that they depended on swimming for safety, something the American Indians and other aboriginals did not do. And, of course, the old U.S. camp standards demanded little that resembled the aboriginal strokes.

It should be reemphasized that, though this volume is only sketchily concerned with canoe camping, it is vitally concerned with camp canoeing. I refer to organized camps. They have done vast amounts of canoe instructing and have generally done it poorly. I have watched organized camp canoeing since 1915 and was a head canoeing counselor for a dozen seasons and an advisor for 10 more. I was never asked to swim and never needed to.

Don't misunderstand me; I believe everyone should be able to swim, but a person need not swim at all in connection with canoeing. North-country natives cannot swim a stroke, and yet they get on fine as canoeists. I have never known either aboriginals or Canadian woods professionals who depended on swimming. If they could swim, they never needed to. Neither have I.

You will note that I pay little attention to swimming in connection with the canoeing of organized camps. The swimming has always gone well in organized camps because it is coached by good swimmers. The canoeing has usually gone badly, for lack of good coaching.

Some of the past standards had serious errors of omission as well as errors of commission. In one set of standards, portaging is mentioned for "discussion." Presumably the compilers had to acknowledge the problem, but they understood it so vaguely that they passed over it. The non-treatment of poling has been largely parallel.

Now, let's do a little creative thinking. Let's try to imagine the standards that an old Indian instructor might have used if he had run an organized camp. Perhaps we will discover some useful approaches to the teaching of canoeing in today's organized camps.

The Standards (Camp or School)

Responsible people should be designated to give canoeing permissions. The paddling boundaries should be assigned, and the times of return should be known within reason.

Paddlers must be classified and listed. If the camp is big, the counselor should have a chart noting the status of every canoeist. This one person should assume all responsibility for every canoeist who uses a canoe on any certain day.

All unqualified paddlers should be kept out of canoes except for instruction. This rule applies especially to *visitors* and *camp employees*.

When canoes are landed, the permittees should promptly check in with the person who gave the canoeists permission to go out.

An unmistakable signal should be used for calling canoes in: big bell, bullhorn, siren, the firing of a blank cartridge. Anything to attract attention clearly. A noise is better than a visual signal such as a flag.

Classification of Paddlers

CLASS D. *Beginners.* May use canoes for instruction only.

CLASS C. *Elementary Canoeists.* May not use a canoe unless accompanied by a responsible counselor.

CLASS B.   *Intermediate Canoeists.* May use canoes with members of their own or higher class under counselor supervision or counselor permission.

CLASS A.   *Advanced Canoeists.* May use canoes alone or under any arrangement with the Head Canoeing Counselor. Similar tests may be considered as qualifying for Assistant Canoeing Counselor.

CLASS AA.   *Head Canoeing Counselor.* In charge of all canoeing.

CLASS AAA.   *Canoeing Examiner.* The highest possible rating and may be somewhat honorary.

All canoeists may well be classified by these camp standards, subject to promotion or demotion. Nothing need be permanent unless earned at least three times during three years or more.

Head Canoeing Counselors should be certified by Canoeing Examiners or by a staff that includes a Canoeing Examiner.

Class D Qualifications

These canoeists are taught forward paddling from a barge or war canoe if either is available. If they use a regular canoe, it must be at least 18 feet long, 36 inches wide, and 13 inches deep amidships (about the size of an 18-foot standard Grumman).

Class C Elementary Canoeist

(Classes C and higher must be organically sound and capable of strenuous exertion).

They must learn the four basic strokes (Forward, Backing, Draw, and Push-over). They must know how to launch and land a canoe, how to keep the canoe clean, and how a beginning paddler should kneel.

In calm water, paddle in tandem (or in a crew of four) at least 2 miles in 40 minutes or less.

Paddle 10 miles during one day.

Class discussion should include general canoeing vocabulary, safety methods, and anything else a Head Canoeing Counselor considers essential.

Class B Intermediate Canoeists

Everything in Class C should be mastered first.

Then, the Stern Steering Stroke, Sweep, and Sculling strokes must be learned.

Simple stunts for balance (such as "jouncing" and gunwale paddling) should be managed at the instructor's discretion.

An Intermediate must "command" a crew of two or four, handle the canoe well, take it out and bring it back safely, and steer around a float not larger than 10 x 15 feet and not cutting the corners by more than 3 feet. This without changing sides with the paddles.

Bow steering must be managed reasonably well.

Using a passenger for ballast, and not changing sides with the paddle, an Intermediate must paddle solo a reasonably straight course ¼ mile and return.

Paddle in tandem at least 20 miles in a day.
Paddle in tandem 5 miles in 75 minutes or less.
Learn the elements of portaging, at least how four canoeists can carry a canoe in their hands. (Boys under age 16 will not be expected to carry canoes alone. Girls will not be expected to carry a canoe alone, although some can.)
Class discussion may well consider anything or everything in this book. Especially safety training.

Class A Advanced Canoeists

This is the highest rating for a camper and lowest for a counselor. Naturally, everything of lower ratings will be mastered previously.

An advanced canoeist should know most or all of the information in this book. He or she must have some teaching ability—enough to teach strokes. I have had good Assistant Canoeing Counselors who could not manage stern steering instruction for backward students. The Head Canoeing Counselor had to help.

On trips, an Assistant must be well up in the "chain of command." Perhaps direct smallish canoe trips. Especially if the camp is big and there is only one Head. I have been the equivalent of an Examiner in a big camp and had three division Heads or equivalent. They were not labeled, just recognized.

Personality counts in everything, and an Assistant must be something of a natural disciplinarian. If canoeists do not obey orders (and I mean *orders!*) there will be danger of serious accidents. The Assistant must order canoeists of lower ratings and must accept orders from superiors. Often there is no time for explanations. No one should give orders without authority. But when given, orders must be obeyed immediately and be unquestioned.

An Assistant, in addition to knowing all the techniques, must also have certain skills and stamina. A man or sizable boy alone should pick up and carry a canoe (65 pounds or heavier) half a mile in 15 minutes or less, not taking a rest, and lay it down correctly. Actually he should do it in 10 minutes with an 85-pound canoe.

But I reiterate: I do not expect girls, or women, or boys under 16 to lug a canoe alone. There can be exceptions. I camped with one 14-year-old boy who could carry an 85-pound canoe uphill for a mile and make time. And I have seen husky Indian women carry canoes as readily as men. I have never seen a woman of any other race portage a canoe alone, but I have no doubt that some could manage it.

An Assistant should also be a poler. Some camps, however, are not near fast water, so this lack of opportunity to learn poling need not prohibit a canoeist from reaching Assistant grade.

Head Canoeing Counselor

A Head Canoeing Counselor is the canoeing dictator in a camp or school. This person must know everything, be both a disciplinarian and teacher. On trips, the Head must be the administrator unless an Examiner is available.

Some standards have emphasized the teaching of large groups. This goal is only nominal without considerable help. Strokes are the absolute essentials, and the only way to perfect them in a student is to take a single subject in a canoe, facing, and demonstrate. Thus, a Head will have to train Assistants. The Assistants teach the details.

When it comes time to run fast water with a 10-canoe party, you have no time for explanations. Canoeists should follow orders. No one should blunder. A blunder may cause an accident.

Canoeing Examiner

I cannot recall more than three or four people who were qualified for this rank. And those I taught myself! Call it egotism or confidence. I hope for an Examiner to know all the basic canoeing that exists. These basics are not long or difficult. They've simply been neglected. Furthermore, he or she must be a teacher of counselors and campers.

An Examiner must also approach canoeing from an anthropological viewpoint. It's not necessary to study anthropology, though this would be desirable. I learned my anthropology through canoe research. But I could not research paddling methods. Nobody had written the details of aboriginal paddling. These I had to write. But the historic canoes and their equipment may be studied extensively.

Perhaps my biggest job as an Examiner (though not so named) concerned canoe safety. Camp directors and swimming heads had devised "Canoe Tests" that had practically no connection with canoeing, except that they involved water. Though these tests were conceived in the noble interests of safety, they actually hampered canoeing instruction.

Canoeing is a simple art that has been widely hampered by organized ignorance. An Examiner should know a few items on canoeing's perimeter. A smattering of anthropology has been emphasized. A bit of physics or engineering has its value.

Camp young people are usually not scientists, but some parents and visitors are. So a canoeing counselor of Examiner grade had better be able to explain the "whys." I don't know all of the mathematics of canoeing, but enough to make the canoe go and enough to answer intelligent questions. All of this suggests that a Canoeing Examiner or even a Head Counselor should know much more than canoeing.

I recall something that happened a decade or more ago. It was the first time my bow gunner, Dr. Karl Holte, and I had jumped mallards going up the rather fast Spring Creek on the Fort Hall Indian Reservation. At the top of a fairly steep pitch, we had grabbed a bush for a breather. Dr. Holte (a botanist) shook his head.

"We can't do it," he said.

"Can't do what?" I asked.

"Go up this creek."

"We're doing it, are we not?" was my reply.

"It's against the laws of physics," he said.

We were both well aware that no one does anything against physical laws. And I am no physicist.

The facts in this situation were interesting. We could paddle maybe 4 miles an hour average in dead water. The stream was flowing at 5 miles per hour.

Yet we were moving about 2 miles per hour against it. Impossible? Not at all.

If my aluminum Grumman had been covered with rough bark, maybe it would have been impossible. But that smooth, streamlined little ship produced slight friction. Furthermore, I hugged the inside of the curves, close to shore, where the current was slowest. I knew the stream and took advantage of every yard of eddy. I poled with my paddle held edgewise in shallow water. And when you're going upstream, it always helps to have a tail wind, which we happened to have that day.

Index